Requirements Management

*This book is dedicated
to all those who do good,
who serve and help others,
who give hope to people in despair,
who provide food and shelter to people in need,
who offer education and opportunities to the poor,
and who promote peace and love in our world today.*

Requirements Management

How to Ensure You Achieve What You Need from Your Projects

MARIO KOSSMANN

GOWER

Published by
Gower Publishing Limited
Wey Court East
Union Road
Farnham
Surrey, GU9 7PT
England

Ashgate Publishing Company
110 Cherry Street
Suite 3-1
Burlington,
VT 05401-3818
USA

www.gowerpublishing.com

British Library Cataloguing in Publication Data
Kossmann, Mario.
  Requirements management : how to ensure you achieve what
  you need from your projects.
  1. Aeronautics--Systems engineering--Management.
  2. Aeronautics--Systems engineering--Quality control.
  3. Industrial procurement--Quality control. 4. Project
  management.
  I. Title
  629.1'34'068-dc23

  ISBN: 978-1-4094-5137-2 (hbk)
  ISBN: 978-1-4094-5138-9 (ebk – PDF)
  ISBN: 978-1-4094-7141-7 (ebk – ePUB)

The Library of Congress has cataloged the printed edition as follows:
Kossmann, Mario.
  Requirements management : how to ensure you achieve what you need from your projects
  / by Mario Kossmann.
    p. cm.
  Includes bibliographical references and index.
  ISBN 978-1-4094-5137-2 (hardback) -- ISBN 978-1-4094-5138-9 (ebook)   1.   Project
  management. I. Title.
  HD69.P75K676 2012
  658.4'04--dc23
                                                                              2012019178

Printed and bound in Great Britain by the
MPG Books Group, UK

Contents

List of Figures   *vii*
List of Tables   *ix*
List of Abbreviations   *xi*
Acknowledgements   *xiii*
About the Author   *xv*
Glossary   *xvii*
Reviews for Requirement Managements   *xxvii*

PART I   INTRODUCTION TO REQUIREMENTS
             MANAGEMENT

Chapter 1   Introduction   3

Chapter 2   RM from a Systems Engineering Perspective   19

Chapter 3   RM from a Project and Program Management
             Perspective   41

PART II   PUTTING REQUIREMENTS MANAGEMENT
             INTO PRACTICE

Chapter 4   Human Factors – The Key to Success   55

Chapter 5   The RM Process   73

Chapter 6   Techniques and Tools Supporting the RM Process 117

Chapter 7   The Use of RM at Three Levels of System Complexity 135

Chapter 8   Conclusion   153

Appendix A: Human Aspects – Dos and Don'ts   157

Appendix B: Process Checklist – Requirements Development (RD)   159

Appendix C: Process Checklist – Requirements Change Management (RCM)   165

Appendix D: Tools Supporting Requirements Management (RD + RCM)   167

Appendix E: Requirements Quality Checklist (Individual Requirements)   169

Appendix F: Requirements Document Quality Checklist (Set Of Requirements)   171

Appendix G: Mapping of RM Workflows to Supporting Techniques and Tools   173

Bibliography   175

Index   177

List of Figures

1.1	Overview of the contents and structure of the book	7
1.2	Classification of non-functional requirements	10
2.1	The Airbus A380	20
2.2	The served system and the serving system	21
2.3	Managing SE data – a typical 'as is' situation	26
2.4	Managing SE data – enhancing reuse of domain knowledge	27
2.5	Managing SE data – combining two development levels	28
2.6	Managing SE data – multiple development levels	28
2.7	A simplified overview of Systems Engineering	30
3.1	An example project schedule (Business Improvement Project)	44
3.2	An example cash flow table and chart (System Development Project)	45
3.3	An example risk register (IS/IT Project)	47
3.4	An example Earned Value Management chart	48
3.5	A simplified overview of Project and Program Management	49
5.1	High-level overview of the generic RM process	75
5.2	The four steps of the generic RM process	76
5.3	Explore the context	78
5.4	Identify the needs	84
5.5	Establish the requirements	89
5.6	A generic goal hierarchy	90
5.7	Manage requirements change	109
7.1	Use of RM for simple systems	137
7.2	More than the Statue of Liberty	138
7.3	The main stakeholders and their needs	139
7.4	Meeting the academic requirements	141
7.5	Use of RM for complex systems	142
7.6	Starting the construction	144
7.7	The main stakeholders and their needs	145
7.8	Completing the school	146

7.9   Use of RM for highly complex systems   147
7.10   The Airbus A350 XWB   148
7.11   The extended enterprise of the A350 XWB program   149
7.12   The simplified A350 XWB requirements cascade   151

List of Tables

4.1	Strategies for dealing with resistance	61
4.2	The eight-stage process of creating major change	63
5.1	Identify and review relevant documentation	79
5.2	Identify and map stakeholders	81
5.3	Elicit and capture relevant context information	83
5.4	Derive needs	85
5.5	Analyze and update needs	87
5.6	Validate needs	88
5.7	Create goal hierarchies	90
5.8	Analyze and update goal hierarchies	92
5.9	Validate goal hierarchies	93
5.10	Write requirements	95
5.11	Parsing requirement statements into components	97
5.12	Example requirement statements	98
5.13	A selection of useful requirement attributes	99
5.14	A requirements document template	102
5.15	Analyze and update requirements	106
5.16	Validate requirements	107
5.17	Identify the need for change	110
5.18	Analyze the impacts of the identified need for change	111
5.19	Prepare the proposed change	113
5.20	Analyze the impacts of the proposed change	114
5.21	Agree the proposed changes	115
5.22	Implement the agreed changes	116
6.1	Main techniques and tools (gathering and structuring information)	127
6.2	Main techniques and tools (tracing information)	130
6.3	Main techniques and tools (analyzing information)	131
6.4	Main techniques and tools (reporting and documenting information)	133

List of Abbreviations

Act   Activity

CM   Configuration Management

COTS   Commercial Off-The-Shelf

DE   Domain Expert

EV   Earned Value

EVM   Earned Value Management

GUI   Graphical User Interface

HMI   Human Machine Interface

HRM   Human Resource Management

KPIs   Key Performance Indicators

NCM   Non-Compliance and Non-Conformance Management

NFRs   Non-functional Requirements

P&PM   Project and Program Management

RCM   Requirements Change Management

RD   Requirements Development

RM   Requirements Management

RS   Relevant Stakeholder

ROM   Risk and Opportunity Management

SE   Systems Engineering

SysML   Systems Modeling Language

UML   Unified Modeling Language

V&V   Validation and Verification

WF   Workflow

Acknowledgements

I would like to express my sincere thanks to all that supported me in one way or another while writing this book, and going through this very interesting, challenging but also rewarding phase of my life.

I would like to express my deepest gratitude to Dr. Vassilis Agouridas (Eurocopter); Dietmar Knauer and Stephen Watts (Airbus); Dr. Mohammed Odeh, Dr. Zaheer Khan and Dr. Kamran Munir (University of the West of England); Younes Al-Hroub (European Bioinformatics Institute); Steve Boughton and Elaine Prescott (QinetiQ); Dr. Clive Bancroft (Enabling Process Technologies); Prof. h.c. cn. Eckhard Michel (International Business Management Consultant); as well as Dr. Arnout Mertens (Salvatorian Office for International Aid), who offered me their very kind and much appreciated support in reviewing the present work from the industrial and academic perspectives, and gave me valuable inputs to improve the consistency of my work.

Also I would like to thank Airbus, Eurocopter, the University of the West of England, the Salvatorian Office for International Aid (SOFIA) and the United Nations (UN) for their kind support and/or material provided.

Of course, I could not have completed my research and written this book if it had not been for the support, love and encouragement of my wife Virginie, and my children Joseph and Loveday.

My thanks also go to my parents and my brothers, as well as many friends from the UK, Germany, France, Spain, Mexico, USA, Puerto Rico, Finland, Italy, Lithuania, Austria, Palestine, Poland, India, Pakistan, Jordan, China, Greece, Iran, the Netherlands, Kenya, Cameroon and the Democratic Republic of the Congo, who gave me their support and strong encouragement at different points in time during these recent and sometimes difficult and exhausting years.

In particular, I would like to thank our dear friends Richard and Dee Hamilton-James for proofreading this book and helping me considerably to improve its readability.

I am very grateful indeed for having had the opportunity to be in touch with, work with, and learn from so many wonderful people around me. May work like this and the related interactions among all involved contribute to helping us humans learn to love and respect one another.

About the Author

 Dr. Mario Kossmann is an experienced Systems Engineer and Capability Integrator for Airbus, having previously worked for Blohm & Voss as Systems Engineer, Technical Manager and also Consultant in Services Marketing. He has served as a naval officer with the German and French navies, and was awarded an MEng in Aerospace Technology from the University of the Federal Armed Forces in Munich (Germany), an MBA from the University of Warwick (UK) and a PhD in Requirements Engineering from the University of the West of England (UK). Mario is the author of the book *Delivering Excellent Service Quality in Aviation* (Ashgate 2006), as well as numerous research publications in the field of Systems Engineering. He is also a certified Project Manager and a Certified Systems Engineering Professional (CSEP). Currently, Mario works as Product Development Process Architect and is conducting research in Ontology-driven Requirements Engineering (OntoREM), Product Family Management (PFM) and Value-Driven Design (VDD).

Glossary

Act (Activity)   An activity is an integrated component of one or several workflows. An activity can potentially be conducted concurrently with a number of different stakeholders (relevant stakeholders and domain experts), and there may be several iterations.

CM (Configuration Management)   Configuration Management is the discipline that focuses on establishing and maintaining consistency of a product or system by ensuring that all related items and their components, as well as any changes to these over time, are known, documented, controlled and tracked.

Cost Management   Cost Management in the context of Project and Program Management is the discipline concerned with planning, controlling and forecasting the recurring and non-recurring costs of a project or program. Cost management is closely linked with the system or product breakdown structure and the related work breakdown structure. The discipline covers the areas of financial accounting and management accounting for the project or program at hand.

COTS (Commercial Off-The-Shelf)   COTS tools in the context of this book are defined to be mature software tools that are available for purchase on the market.

DE (Domain Expert)   A domain expert is a stakeholder or an unconcerned, who might not even be part of the project or program in question, but who has relevant expertise or experience in the field at hand.

Design   Design in the context of Systems Engineering is the discipline that is concerned with finding existing or generating new solutions to satisfy the established system requirements, usually within a given project or program.

Design activities cover many activities from early concept development and selection, via the detailed specification of solution architecture and its intended production and assembly, to the integration of subsystem components into the overall system.

EV (Earned Value) Earned Value is the value of work that was performed for a component of the work breakdown structure of a project, in a specific period of time. Earned value is usually contrasted with the planned value of the work that was planned to be performed for the same component of the work breakdown structure, in the same period of time. Earned value may also be contrasted to the actual cost incurred for the work performed for the component of the work breakdown structure in question, in the same period of time.

EVM (Earned Value Management) Earned Value Management is a project management technique that enables ongoing tracking of the project progress made in terms of earned value as opposed to the planned progress, or the actual cost incurred – all for the same work for a given component of the work breakdown structure in a specific period of time. Earned value may be tracked on a weekly or monthly basis or at important milestones of a given project. The identified cost incurred and time spent for progress achievement can both be compared against the planning. This enables a decision to be made on corrective actions in the short term, and predictions made for cost controlling purposes. For example, the total project cost at completion can be predicted using this approach for the entire project.

Formal 'Formal' here means in accordance with a pre-established set of definitions, procedures, notations or languages in order to enable machine-readability and facilitate analysis.

Goal A goal is an informal expression of how one or several aspects of an identified need are intended to be satisfied. Each need, if followed up, will lead to the development of a goal hierarchy consisting of several goals and sub-goals. Within such a goal hierarchy, a goal is considered to be satisfied when all its derived sub-goals are satisfied. Those goals that cannot further be broken down into sub-goals are called root goals. Requirements will be established for root goals only, not for any other goals that are not root goals. If all root goals within a goal hierarchy are satisfied, the underlying need of this goal hierarchy is considered to be satisfied.

GUI (Graphical User Interface)   A Graphical User Interface is a key human user interface within computer based systems.

HMI (Human Machine Interface)   Human Machine Interfaces, formerly known as Man Machine Interfaces (MMI), address the human user interfaces within systems, for example, graphical user interfaces.

HRM (Human Resource Management)   Human Resource Management in the context of Project and Program Management is the discipline concerned with planning and controlling the availability of the human resources needed in order to successfully carry out a project or program. This discipline is closely linked to the work breakdown structure and schedule of the project or program.

KPIs (Key Performance Indicators)   Key Performance Indicators are a set of meaningful, qualitative or quantitative values that are regularly measured, or calculated based on measurements against defined criteria, in order to enable or enhance process control, continuous improvement and management decision-making in a given context.

Material Resource Management   Material Resource Management in the context of Project and Program Management is the discipline concerned with planning and putting in place the material resources needed for the successful completion of a project or program. This discipline is closely linked to the system or product breakdown structure, the work breakdown structure and the schedule of the project or program.

Model   Models are simplified representations of complex reality, designed to support technical activities such as requirements elicitation; analysis and validation; design activities, including design verification; product integration and verification; product validation; as well as training and marketing. There are many different kinds of models.

Modeling   Modeling is the process of generating and using models.

Monitoring and Control   Monitoring and Control in the context of Project and Program Management is the discipline concerned with continuously checking progress made against the established project plan, and identifying any actual or potential deviations from it by means of relevant Key Performance Indicators. The main purpose of this discipline is to highlight emerging risks and issues, and signal when corrective actions are necessary.

NCM (Non-Compliance and Non-Conformance Management) Non-Compliance and Non-Conformance Management in the context of Systems Engineering is the discipline that is concerned with the systematic management of non-compliances and non-conformances.

Need A need is the informal expression of something that has to be provided, ensured or avoided by a system or the development project of this system, from the viewpoint of one or several stakeholders. Needs are derived from the specified problem space of a given domain or project, that is, they are based on specific problem areas or aspects. This problem space of a given domain or project has to be specified with the help of the identified relevant stakeholders and domain experts. Each need, if followed up, will lead to the development of a goal hierarchy.

NFRs (Non-functional Requirements) Requirements that describe non-functional properties of a system, or of one or several of its components.

Non-Compliance A non-compliance is given when a design solution does not comply with the underlying requirements. It is usually identified during the design verification activities and will lead either to a change of the design solution or the requirements, or alternatively to an accepted deviation that possibly leads to a limitation of the product or system. Any such deviations or resulting limitations will have to be agreed with the relevant stakeholders.

Non-Conformance A non-conformance is given when a product or system does not conform with the underlying requirements and/or the design. It is usually identified during the product verification activities, or in some cases during the operational life of a system. It will result either in a necessary change of the product or system, or alternatively a concession and/or a limitation. Any such concessions or limitations will have to be agreed with the relevant stakeholders.

Ontology The word 'ontology' comes from the Greek words *ontos* (for 'being') and *logos* (for 'word') and traditionally refers to the subject of existence in philosophy. A domain ontology explains or specifies all concepts and their relations within a given domain. It defines the domain terminology (vocabulary) and taxonomy including hierarchies of classes, instances, properties and axioms. It is generated, validated and maintained over time by the members and stakeholders of a given domain, and aims to be both understandable by humans and machine-readable.

P&PM (Project and Program Management) Project and Program Management is the discipline concerned with the management of projects or programs. Project management includes requirements management, project establishment, monitoring and control, schedule management, cost management, human resource management, material resource management, risk and opportunity management, supplier management, earned value management, as well as project closure and handover. In addition to that, program management has to define and implement business strategy, and steer a set of related or embedded projects and recurring processes during the entire life cycle of a system, with the aim to generate some stakeholder benefits such as profit.

Process A process is an organized set of workflows and related activities which transform inputs into outputs. Process descriptions or models are essential to be able to reuse and continuously improve knowledge in general, and the defined processes themselves in particular.

Program A program intends to deliver a specific business case, which usually includes revenues from external sources and profit to the company. It spans across the total life cycle of a system or product, coordinates a set of technical, administrative and financial tasks, intended to develop, produce and support a system for the benefit of the stakeholders. It consists of a set of related or embedded projects, and recurring processes. A program is managed in a coordinated way in order to obtain business benefits and control that would otherwise not be achievable by merely managing the related projects in isolation.

Project A project is a unique and temporary process consisting of a set of coordinated and controlled workflows and related activities with a specific duration, as well as explicit start and finish dates. A project is undertaken to achieve a set of unique objectives, although the final outcome of how these objectives will be met are likely not to be known exactly from the outset of a project. Each project will be subject to a set of requirements that often will have to be developed as part of the project, as well as a number of other constraints such as budget, schedule and resource availability. Projects may be categorized into system development or modification projects, business improvement projects, information system or information technology (IS/IT) projects, and research projects.

Requirement   A requirement is a detailed expression of specific aspects of a less detailed stakeholder need, via the elaborated root goals of the latter. It formalizes a relationship between one or several stakeholders and the developer of a system. Requirements are most frequently expressed as textual requirements, but in some areas, such as safety critical software requirements, formal requirements or models may be used. Requirements are descriptions of how a system should behave (functional requirements), or of an overall system property or attribute (non-functional requirements). They may be a constraint on the development process, and on the program or project by which the system in question will be developed or modified.

RCM (Requirements Change Management) Requirements Change Management is the process of managing changes to requirements over the entire life cycle of a system or program. The principal requirements change management activities are change control and change impact assessment. Requirements change management requires traceability information to be recorded such as specific links among requirements, the sources of requirements, the system design, and planned actions and evidence of validation and verification activities.

RD (Requirements Development)   Requirements Development is the process of developing requirements. It can be subdivided into a number of potentially concurrent and iterative phases: Elicitation, Analysis and Negotiation, Documentation and Validation. The output of this process is a set of validated requirements.

Requirements Manager A Requirements Manager is a generic role that conducts requirements management, including both requirements development and requirements change management over time. Depending on the given context, this role may be played by an individual who plays several development roles in simple system contexts, or by a dedicated and experienced RM professional in case of highly complex system development contexts.

RM (Requirements Management) Requirements Management is the discipline concerned with elaborating the requirements for a given project, program, or system to be developed in a given context, based on the needs of all relevant stakeholders, analyzing and negotiating these requirements, tracing them, validating them with the relevant stakeholders and managing their change over time. RM consists of requirements development (RD) from elicitation or reuse to validation and requirements change management (RCM) over time.

Role   A role is a generic set of assigned responsibilities for specific process elements. A role may be performed by one dedicated person, or alternatively by a group of people jointly, or by an individual who also performs one or several other roles at the same time.

ROM (Risk and Opportunity Management)   Risk and Opportunity Management in the context of Project and Program Management is the discipline concerned with identifying, categorizing, prioritizing, mitigating (where appropriate for risks), exploiting (where appropriate for opportunities) and tracking any identified risks or opportunities that are relevant for a given project or program.

RS (Relevant Stakeholder)   Relevant stakeholders are those stakeholders among the many possible stakeholders that have been designated to be the official stakeholders within a given project or program. The relevant stakeholders usually have to sign off the requirements after they have been validated.

Scenario   A scenario describes an operational or other life cycle context, during which a system is required to show a specific behavior or have a specific characteristic or quality. Exploring the different relevant scenarios during the development of a new system, in particular during the requirements elicitation, helps to appropriately limit the validity of individual requirements, and contributes to ensuring the overall completeness of the requirements.

Schedule Management   Schedule Management in the context of Project and Program Management is the discipline concerned with planning all identified work activities throughout the project or program. The discipline is closely linked to the work breakdown structure of the project or program.

SE (Systems Engineering)   Systems Engineering is an interdisciplinary approach to develop systems. It entails a number of technical disciplines such as Requirements Management, Design, Manufacturing, Validation and Verification, and Configuration Management that enable the systematic development of systems. The processes of these disciplines, and the information that is created and communicated as part of these, need to be maintained over the entire life cycle of a system, and have to be interfaced, integrated and made traceable via SE.

Service   The generation of an essentially intangible benefit, either on its own or as part of a tangible product or system, which satisfies an identified stakeholder need.

Stakeholder   Stakeholders are individuals, groups or organizations who will be affected in some way by the development, sale, delivery, support, operational use or disposal of a system to be developed, and therefore have a direct or indirect influence on the system requirements. They include end-users of the system, clients who are paying for the system, managers and others involved in the organizational processes influenced by the system; engineers responsible for the system development and maintenance; customers of the organization, who will use the system to provide some services; external bodies such as regulators or certification authorities, and so on. Often, the distinction is made between external stakeholders that are outside the boundaries of a given organization or company; and internal stakeholders that are part of the organization or company in question.

Supplier Management   Supplier Management in the context of Project and Program Management is the discipline concerned with planning and managing all non-technical aspects of subcontracting work packages within the extended enterprise. In the context of a given project or program, the extended enterprise consists of the own company, as well as the selected risk sharing partners, suppliers, and subcontractors.

SysML (Systems Modeling Language)   The Systems Modeling Language is a modeling notation or specification language that was developed based on the Unified Modeling Language (UML), but that was specifically adapted for the enhanced use in the Systems Engineering context.

System   A system can be defined as an integrated set of interacting elements such as products, services, people, processes, hardware, software, firmware and information. A system serves a defined purpose. A system may consist of a number of integrated subsystems ('system of systems'), and may be integrated itself into a wider system (the 'served system').

Technique   A technique is a method or specific set of activities to carry out a process or workflow using one or several tools.

Tool   A tool is a physical or software means that enables, supports or facilitates one or several activities or workflows.

Traceability   Traceability means the ability to trace related information objects such as sources of requirements, requirements and V&V data, for example, by means of links or traceability matrices, in order to enable different types of analyses and the controlled reuse of these information objects. Traceability is key to being able to exploit the information that is generated and managed during the RM process. Forward requirements traceability means the traceability from sources of requirements towards the resulting requirements. Backwards requirements traceability means the traceability from the requirements back to their sources. Traceability can be enriched by introducing different types of links and also relationships between several links.

UML (Unified Modeling Language)   The Unified Modeling Language is a modeling notation or specification language that was developed based on international diagramming conventions for the context of Software Engineering.

Use Case   A use case describes one or several related and purposeful interactions between a human person or an external system (or element thereof) with the system of interest. In a given use case, a system may be required to show a specific behavior or have a specific characteristic or quality. Exploring the different relevant use cases during the development of a new system, in particular during the requirements elicitation, helps to appropriately limit the validity of individual requirements, and contributes to ensuring the overall completeness of the requirements

V&V (Validation and Verification)   Validation and Verification is an overlapping discipline that covers requirements validation, design verification and product verification; although the requirements validation is part of the requirements management process, and design verification is part of the design process. V&V aims to ensure that (1) the requirements are sufficiently correct, complete and consistent based on the identified stakeholder needs, (2) the system design satisfies the requirements and (3) the system or product satisfies both the requirements and the design. V&V thereby helps to reduce development risks and corrective rework.

Viewpoint   A viewpoint is a collection of system, problem or context related information about a domain, which is held by an individual stakeholder or domain expert. The overall set of system requirements has to take into account the different viewpoints of the identified relevant stakeholders and domain experts.

WF (Workflow) A workflow consists of a number of related activities. A workflow can potentially be conducted concurrently with a number of different stakeholders, that is, relevant stakeholders and domain experts, and there may be several iterations of a workflow.

Reviews for
Requirements Management

There are many books and scientific publications on systems engineering and requirements management. This book is not claiming to substitute them but rather offers a comprehensive and practical guide for project managers in a wide range of business contexts of different levels of complexity. The book is written in a simple but not simplistic manner supported by concrete and detailed real life examples, thereby allowing non-experts in the field to greatly enhance their project outcomes via improved management of their requirements.

Dr. Vassilis Agouridas, Strategy & Company Development,
Eurocopter

I believe this book contains nuggets of gold that when understood, adopted and applied will improve my performance as both a leader and consultant and also that of my company.

Dr. Clive Bancroft, Managing Director,
Enabling Process Technologies

A set of inspiring requirements management reflections by a senior requirements engineer and process architect with very rich experience over more than a decade in the field.

Dr. Mohammed Odeh, Head of Software Engineering Research
Group, University of the West of England

This book is a practical and easy-to-follow guide for best practice on an underestimated topic: we often do not get what we really need from projects, and yet we seem to be reluctant to change that, because we erroneously think we haven't got the time. I strongly recommend this book, it's an eye-opener.

Prof. h.c. cn. Eckhard Michel,
International Business Management Consultant

PART I

Introduction to Requirements Management

1

Introduction

Chapter Summary

This first chapter answers some initial questions you may have, in particular why you should read this book and how you can use it most effectively and efficiently, depending on your own background and business context. This will help you to save time and focus on the most urgent aspects that you need to know about in your current situation. Then the chapter explains the nature, use and importance of requirements, and introduces the discipline of Requirements Management (RM).

Why You Should Read This Book

Most people will have had negative experience when they needed something but were delivered something else they did not need, or that did not fully satisfy their needs. Not getting what you really need usually leads to disappointment and frustration. In many business contexts this is likely to waste time and money, leading to delays, budget overruns and, in the worst case, project failure.

In some safety-critical or charity-related fields, not satisfying the real needs may well lead directly to loss of life and immense human suffering – for example, if the water distribution system for an overcrowded refugee camp was not properly specified, and as a result, an unsatisfactory system was purchased and flown into the crisis area.

In many cases, in particular in our private lives in more affluent and wealthy societies, the consequences may not be so dire, but people may still spend a lot of money on a new heating system for their house that does not really meet their needs, or they may purchase the wrong family car, or invest their bonus in the wrong holiday package for their family.

This book does not claim to be an academic publication. Rather, it is a practical and realistic guide for anyone who wishes to make his requirements explicit, in order to ensure that his needs are fully met – irrespective of the industry, the sector (public or private), the purpose of the organization (profit or not-for-profit), and the general context (work or leisure). The contents of this book are the results of a large variety of applied research, good practice, and hands-on experience across many industries.

How to Use This Book

This book directly addresses you as a reader and potential user of the proposed approach to RM. The assumptions taken would be that you are in a specific situation, in which (a) you as a 'customer' either have to make explicit what you need in order to make the right purchase decision, or to have something developed and made for you; or (b) you as a 'provider' will have to ensure that you have identified all customer requirements before you provide your customer with what he really needs.

In the former case, you may be looking for a new house or a car to buy; in the latter case you may be an architect or own a building company or car dealership.

Regarding your experience, you may have had negative experience with not getting what you really needed when you made a major buy decision, or you may be an experienced professional requirements manager or project manager, and you want to improve the way you develop and work with requirements.

In many business contexts, especially in the public sector including the defence sector, there are multiple standards that have to be followed in order to develop systems and conduct RM. This book will help you to improve the quality of your requirements and reduce the time to develop and maintain them, while following any mandatory standards.

Whatever your background, experience and business purpose, this book offers you flexible advice and guidance, depending on your own individual needs. If you start working as a requirements manager, you may want to apply the proposed approach in its entirety to your working context. On the other hand, if you already have a lot of experience with requirements, you will find specific parts of the book helpful to improve at least certain aspects of your current approach to developing and managing requirements.

Depending on your own context and experience, as well as your current activities and the necessary level of your own direct involvement in RM, we will look at three distinct types of situation, in which you may find yourself: you will either have sufficient time to go through the entire approach to RM in detail (Case 1), you may only have limited time to look at the proposed approach (Case 2), or you may be under a lot of time pressure and urgently need to get a grip on your requirements (Case 3).

In any case, you can always go back to this guide and revisit certain aspects you may have initially ignored because of the situation you were in. The book is structured in a way that allows you maximum flexibility in terms of how you use it over time.

CASE 1: YOU HAVE THE TIME TO LOOK AT THE PROPOSED APPROACH TO RM IN DETAIL

Please go through the entire book chapter by chapter. This will give you the best insight into the proposed approach to RM and prepare you well for any requirements related work you may have to do in your own context.

CASE 2: YOU HAVE ONLY LIMITED TIME TO LOOK AT THE PROPOSED APPROACH

You will find it useful to read the short chapter summaries at the end of this section (or at the beginning of each chapter) to have a quick overview and decide what seems to be the most relevant chapter for you to read in your given situation. Figure 1.1 provides an overview of the structure of this book in the form of a mind map. All chapters can be read in isolation or in a different order, if this is more helpful to you.

CASE 3: YOU HAVE NO TIME AND URGENTLY NEED TO GET A GRIP ON YOUR REQUIREMENTS

If you urgently have to look into any specific requirements issues and have no time to look properly at the proposed approach in detail, you can go directly to the appendices section of the book and pick the appropriate process checklist. These process checklists provide a summary overview of the recommended activities with their inputs and outputs, as well as indications as to who should participate in these activities.

Also, you could use the requirements quality checklist (for individual requirements) and the requirements document quality checklist (for sets of requirements) to evaluate the quality of your requirements as they are at the moment, and identify areas of needed improvement.

However, it is worthwhile to go through the relevant section of Chapter 5 that describes the phase of the RM process, in which you currently are. The beginning of the chapter gives an overview of the entire process that will allow you to identify the right section you should read. You might also find Figure 1.1 helpful to quickly spot the relevant parts of the book you should concentrate on in the light of your specific situation.

In any case, investing time to get a grip on your requirements will actually save you time, provide you clear visibility and better control over what is happening in your project, and give you a good chance of meeting the underlying needs of your project.

The main body of the book is divided into two parts: Part I is concerned with introducing key aspects of RM, giving an overview of the discipline and explaining why RM is of fundamental importance to the success of any project, whereas Part II is concerned with how RM can actually be put into practice in a large variety of business contexts of different degrees of complexity.

Within the first part, Chapter 1 introduces you to this book, answering some initial questions you may have, and provides some guidance on how to use the book depending on your individual background and context in order to help you save time and focus on the most relevant aspects you need to know about. Based on this introduction, RM is put into its wider context in terms of Systems Engineering (SE) and Project and Program Management (P&PM). Chapter 2 puts RM into the context of SE, defining what is understood by the term 'System' and by the SE approach, explaining why SE is important and what role RM plays as an integral part of SE. Chapter 3 puts RM into the context of P&PM, explaining the difference between projects and programs, defining the discipline of P&PM, explaining why this discipline is important and what role RM plays as an integral part of P&PM.

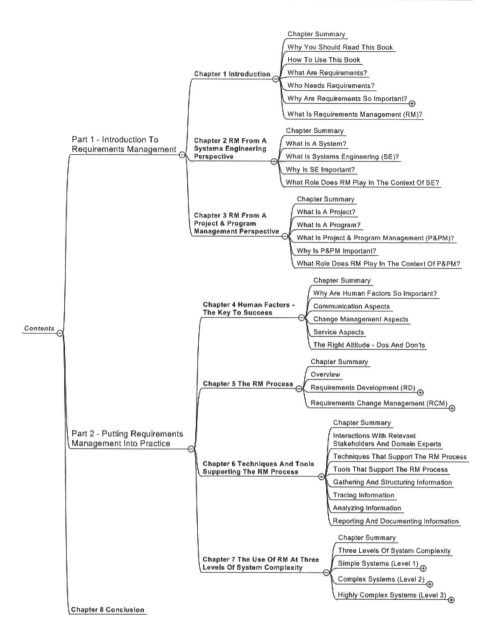

Figure 1.1 Overview of the contents and structure of the book

In the second part of the book about putting RM into practice, Chapter 4 describes essential human factors that should not be underestimated, since these will have to be properly addressed in order to successfully deploy a new RM process in any organization. Then Chapter 5 provides a detailed description of all aspects of the proposed RM process, followed by the description of RM techniques and tools that support this process in Chapter 6.

Although the above three chapters are written in generic terms, the underlying assumption is that the RM process as presented is to be used for the development of a complex or highly complex system. This means that for simple systems, many of the proposed activities will be much less time-consuming and the needed tools to support the process and manage the created data may be less sophisticated, since the data volumes can be expected to be significantly lower.

Chapter 7 explores the application of RM at different levels of system complexity, and provides detailed and graphical insights into three representative example cases. It will help you understand in what category of context you are yourself, and therefore allow you to select the appropriate level of detail and formalism of the RM approach that you should apply in your specific circumstances.

Finally, Chapter 8 concludes with a summary of the main recommendations of how you can implement the content of the book in your own environment and specific context.

Throughout the book, specific examples are used that offer concrete instances of what is described in more generic terms. This aims to enhance your understanding and make the book as helpful as possible for a large variety of readers, who may not necessarily have much experience in all areas covered by the book. Also, the following additional material is provided in the appendices of the book: a human aspects checklist (Dos and Don'ts), key process checklists for requirements development (RD) and requirements change management (RCM), a list of recommended RM tools, a requirements quality checklist, a requirements document quality checklist, as well as a mapping from the RM process workflows to the recommended techniques and tools that can best support them.

What Are Requirements?

For every project, there are usually several stakeholders, that is, people with a vested interest in the project and its outcomes. Each of these stakeholders has certain high-level needs that have to be satisfied by the project and its outcomes for the project to be successful. Some key aspects of these needs have to be elaborated in more detail and made explicit in order to influence the project in a way that the project and its outcomes actually satisfy these stakeholder needs.

Requirements are detailed expressions of specific aspects of less detailed stakeholder needs. They formalize relationships between the stakeholders or customers of a system, and the developers or suppliers of this system. A system here is defined as an integrated set of interacting elements – such as products, services, people, processes, hardware, software, firmware and information – that serves a defined purpose.

Requirements are most frequently expressed as textual requirements, but in some areas such as safety-critical software requirements, formal mathematical requirements or models may be used. Requirements can be descriptions of how a system should behave (functional requirements), or of an overall system property or attribute (non-functional requirements). Other requirements may be a constraint on the development process or project of the system development.

Depending on the business context, there are many different ways of how requirements can be categorized into different types. In the context of software engineering, Sommerville proposed the classification of non-functional requirements shown in Figure 1.2 [1].

Requirements are likely to be of different priority for a given project or program. This priority may be considered in terms of three categories of priority: 'order winners' or 'essential' requirements; 'qualifiers' or 'important' requirements; and 'less important' or 'nice to have' requirements.

The first category covers requirements that have to be satisfied in order to enable the system to stand out as superior over competitors' systems. In cases where there is no competition between alternative systems, this level of priority means that the corresponding key requirements have to be satisfied for the project to be successful. The second category includes requirements that have to be met in order for the system to be even considered as a viable option or alternative. The third category includes requirements that do not necessarily have to be met by the system, although this would be desirable.

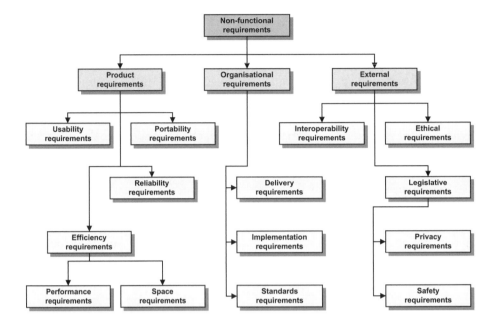

Figure 1.2   Classification of non-functional requirements (adapted from Sommerville, 2007) [1]

Over time, both the requirements themselves and their relative priority may change. This could be the case when specific user needs change or the market in general changes. However, there are two general types of changes: those that are brought about by changes of stakeholder needs, and those that are necessary because the requirements had not been developed to the right level of quality initially, that is, when corrective rework is needed to get the requirements right. The first type of change cannot be avoided and needs to be enabled in a systematic manner; but the second type of change has to be reduced as far as possible, since it causes additional, unplanned delays and costs, without adding any value to the system development.

There are a number of particularly volatile requirements that deserve special attention during the life cycle of a system; in particular, requirements around the interaction between subsystems that are to be integrated into one overarching system of subsystems. Often, when the system is designed at high level, some of the necessary subsystems are not designed or unknown at that time. Once these subsystems are integrated into the overall system, they may show a number of emerging, frequently unintended or at least unexpected properties.

In a business context, requirements are often developed and managed over time by dedicated requirements managers. In such cases, the requirements are not usually owned by the requirements manager, but rather by the people on behalf of whom the requirements manager develops and maintains the requirements. Requirements bridge the gap between the people who have a problem, that is, external and internal stakeholders, and the people who can design and build a suitable solution to the problems at hand. Requirements are also the basis of testing, qualification, risk management, as well as project and program management in general.

Who Needs Requirements?

Anyone who is about to enter or already is in a customer-provider-relationship potentially has requirements to request or provide a system of some sort as a solution to a given set of problems. However, the needed level of detail, granularity and formality of the requirements depends on the given context.

From the customer viewpoint, a large variety of individuals, teams or organizations across industries depend on requirements, in order to specify in detail what their needs are, be it in the private or public sector, within a profit or not-for-profit organization and for a work or leisure context.

From the provider viewpoint, on the other hand, some individual, team or organization providing a solution to satisfy the needs of somebody else, requirements are used to specify clearly the problems that have to be solved by this solution.

Taking both viewpoints into consideration, the requirements become the means to communicate unambiguously and in as much detail as necessary between the customer and the provider. They serve to make explicit, discuss and agree what is needed, that is, what are the problems that have to be solved by the system.

The requirements will have to be baselined so that any changes to the system in the future can be reviewed against the established set of agreed requirements for change impact analysis. Requirements usually become the technical content of the terms of a contractual relationship between a customer and a provider.

For example, the architect of a house may be the customer and a building company may be the provider. In a different industry, the governmental procurement agency may be the customer for a new fighter jet aircraft for the national air force, and an aerospace company may be the provider. In a not-for-profit context, the United Nations (UN) may be the customer for a maritime embargo system off the coast of a particular country that suffers from civil war, and NATO (the North Atlantic Treaty Organization) may be the provider organization of this system in line with the UN requirements.

Why Are Requirements So Important?

From the customer's viewpoint, the agreed set of validated requirements has to clearly specify what problems have to be solved by the system that will be developed by the provider, and under which constraints, otherwise the customer will not get what he needs, when he needs it, and at the price he is willing or able to pay.

From the provider's viewpoint, the agreed set of validated requirements for the development of a given system is the very basis of the development of this system. The requirements are the 'cornerstone' for the project or program developing and supporting the system at hand. Nothing should be developed that is not 'required' by these requirements, or the provider will work on things that are not necessary, that is, he will waste time and money while over-engineering the solution.

On the other hand, all that is required will be addressed by the system to be developed, or the latter will not satisfy the stakeholder needs. And if the provider fails to satisfy the stakeholder needs, the system will probably not be deployed – and, very importantly in a business context, it will not be paid for.

Also, during the life cycle of a system there will probably be many changes to the system. All proposed changes will have to be considered, analyzed, decided, implemented and tested against the established baseline of requirements, or the provider does not know what he is doing, how long it will take, how much it will cost him, and what price he will be able to offer to the customer.

Alexander and Stevens [2] argue that 'if a system designer reaches for the wrong goal, everything he does will be wrong. A single wrong requirement is likely to create a shower of design mistakes.'

Hooks [3] claims that program cost overruns and schedule delays are to a large part associated with requirements problems, ranging from 'incomplete, inconsistent, and incomprehensible requirements to the complexities of the change management process'. She identifies two basic underlying causes of these problems, that is, the 'inability to write good requirements and a lack of understanding about the importance of requirements'. Both causes are 'compounded by the scope, complexity, and long life cycle of major programs'.

There is a clear trend that an increasing number of companies across many industries are attempting to significantly reduce, if not eliminate, corrective rework. They have recognized that high levels of corrective rework hinder or even prevent them from successfully facing today's market trends and customer expectations. Furthermore, during an economic recession, companies that have successfully reduced their levels of corrective rework tend to be more resilient.

Corrective rework, as opposed to improvements, usually adds to costs and delays, as (per definition) it is not budgeted and scheduled in the initial system development plan. Furthermore, high levels of corrective rework invariably have a strong negative influence on the motivation of the people that are involved in the work.

Therefore, the reduction of corrective rework must be among any company's priorities. Developing high quality requirements in terms of correctness, completeness and consistency is a major driver to enable the reduction of corrective rework.

What is Requirements Management (RM)?

Requirements Management is the discipline concerned with elaborating the requirements for a given project, program, or system to be developed in a given context, based on the needs of all relevant stakeholders, analysing and negotiating these requirements, tracing them, validating them with the relevant stakeholders and managing their change over time. RM consists of RD, from elicitation or reuse of requirements to their validation by the relevant stakeholders, and RCM over time, that is, throughout the entire life cycle of a project, program or system.

RD is the process of developing requirements. It can be subdivided into a number of potentially concurrent and iterative phases: Elicitation, Analysis and Negotiation, Documentation and Validation. The output of this process is a set of validated requirements.

RCM is the process of managing changes to requirements over the entire program, project or system life cycle, that is, from the moment requirements are established for the first time during the development process to the disposal of the system at the end of its operational life, or the end of the corresponding program.

The principal RCM activities are change control and change impact assessment. RM requires traceability information to be recorded, in particular links between the requirements and the sources of these requirements, the system design, and planned actions and evidence of validation and verification activities.

RM cannot completely prevent but can at least help to reduce the following: (1) over-specification leading to increased Non-Recurring Costs (NRC) and Recurring Costs (RC); (2) under-specification leading to customer dissatisfaction; and (3) mis-specification leading to unplanned rework or modifications. All three issues clearly have negative effects on the system quality, as well as the project schedule and budget.

We should not be confused by the fact that in some business environments, in particular in the fields of software engineering and IT in general, RM is known as 'Requirements Engineering' and RCM is called 'Requirements Management' over time. One reason why the term 'Requirements Engineering' was not widely adopted in engineering-driven organizations is because these organizations often show a strong divide between traditional functions such as 'Engineering', 'Marketing', 'Finance', 'Customer Support', 'Human Resources' and so on – with 'non-engineering' functions not feeling concerned by the discipline of 'Requirements Engineering' simply because the term contains the word 'Engineering'.

Initially starting in software development, the last decades showed ever increasing use of RM in many technology driven industry sectors such as IT, aerospace, defence, pharmaceutical, automotive, and telecommunications. In particular in the defence sector, multiple standards have evolved on how military systems have to be developed in terms of SE including RM.

The scope of the requirements dealt with has been constantly widened. So in addition to performance, safety and functional requirements, the scope also increasingly includes target cost, quality, confidentiality, environmental and other non-functional requirements. Similarly, the scope of the systems for which requirements are developed and managed has increased from 'products only' towards including 'enabling products' that are needed to develop, produce, market and operationally support these products, as well as other project- and program-related processes.

There are many publications about projects that went wrong for various reasons, the majority of which are connected to a lack of RM or bad implementation of RM [2, 3, 4]. However, although there seems to be consensus that requirements need to be properly elaborated and taken as the basis of the development work of any complex system [5, 6, 7, 8, 9] a significant number of project or program managers and other senior decision-makers still think of RM as an activity that takes place with limited resources at the beginning of a project only.

There is strong evidence that (a) if you know what your customers need, (b) if you keep in touch with them and proactively allow for changes of their needs over time and (c) if you have traceability between your requirements and your design so that you can actually analyze the impact of any changes that will occur during the life cycle, then you are in a much better position to develop successful systems, earn money doing so and gain sustainable competitive advantage over time [10].

Chatzoglou and Macaulay [11] found that RM is an iterative process. In their study 18 per cent of the projects that were considered performed just one iteration, 32 per cent performed two, and 50 per cent performed three or more iterations. Furthermore, they found that the more time is spent on the RM stage, the less time is spent on the entire development process. Also, the higher the cost of the RM stage is, the lower is the cost of the whole development process.

Bahill and Henderson [4] offer good and bad examples of famous systems where RD, validation and verification were undertaken correctly and incorrectly respectively in order to highlight the importance of these activities for the successful realization of systems. The range of famous failures they analyzed includes the *Titanic*, the Tacoma Narrows Bridge, the Vietnam War, *Apollo 13*, Concorde, and the Space Shuttles *Challenger* and *Columbia*.

Lucchetta, Baroni, Delaire and Bariani [12] investigated the importance of RM in the context of aircraft development, using the example of Airbus. They conclude that the design cycle of an aircraft is longer than the fast-changing needs of customers within the air transportation environment, and that the 'robustness of architectural aircraft design during the concept phase against moving requirements throughout the product development is critical for the final, long-term success of the product'. Fricke and Schulz [13] had similar findings in the automotive industry and offer an approach to cope with changeability in their context.

RM continues to face challenges, especially in large, transnational organizations, which are engineering-focused and produce complex, long-lead-time products and services in multidisciplinary contexts. Recent publications have identified difficulties to deploy the RM process in such environments; and maintain the process over time [14, 15]. As a result, requirements are often immature and of low quality, the RM process is likely to take longer than planned, and hence, will be more costly than originally budgeted for. This, in turn, will severely affect the successful completion of projects or programs. Also, essential resources are retained longer in delayed programs and, therefore, they may not be available as planned for other new programs [14, 15].

Work has been undertaken to explore knowledge-driven RM as opposed to merely process-driven RM in the context of the OntoREM project – a joint research project between the University of the West of England and Airbus. Within this project, an Ontology-driven Requirements Engineering Methodology was developed in order to explore the potential benefits of such an approach over traditional RM approaches, by means of case studies in the aerospace industry [16]. Based on this work, a more knowledge-driven approach to RM seems to offer significant potential to produce better quality requirements, faster and cheaper.

Following a more knowledge-driven approach moves the focus from process steps for defined deadlines (but often immature deliverables) to the knowledge needed, from which the deliverables will flow when feasible. There is a lot of documented but unpublished (for commercial reasons) evidence indicating that the traditional process-driven approach leads to significant corrective rework, additional costs and delays.

The knowledge-driven approach will not require as much rework because misunderstandings are reduced, and activities are driven not by unrealistic deadlines but by the availability of relevant knowledge. This enables reuse of both requirements and design solutions, including relevant validation and verification data. However, this seems to be more difficult to project-manage with current P&PM tools [15].

The comprehensive approach to RM that is proposed in this book represents a more knowledge-driven approach that is based on the capture and validation of underlying domain knowledge, and explicitly allows for the iterative and concurrent 'reality' of RM.

In a specific context and for a given team or organization, RM is conducted by the generic role of the Requirements Manager. Depending on the context, this role may be performed by one individual who plays at the same time several development roles in a simple system context, or by a dedicated and experienced RM professional in the case of a complex system development context.

The requirements manager proactively drives the development of the requirements until validation, and then their change management through the entire life cycle of a system. This entails asking the relevant domain experts and stakeholders the right questions, in order to elicit their relevant knowledge and identify their real needs, capturing this knowledge and developing requirements from it, as well as driving validation by the relevant stakeholders.

Also, at least in the case of larger organizations, the deployed RM processes will be under systematic continuous improvement, and corresponding feedback needs to be communicated to the relevant central organization that is continuously working on the RM process, as well as on the supporting data model and tooling.

In many companies, there is a prevalent attitude that if there is a deployed RM 'tool', that is, a commercial software tool that enhances the management of RM-related data, plus a 'tool person' working in the tool and a 'project manager' who controls it all, it is going to be fine. It is often forgotten that RM is a crucial discipline that requires experienced experts in the field to actually apply it to a given business context effectively and efficiently. RM is a profession, not just a 'job to be done in a tool'. At least in larger organizations, professional requirements managers are essential, just as are professional designers and professional project managers.

RM as a discipline is difficult to consider in complete isolation, because it has to interface with a multitude of related disciplines, domains and functions throughout the life cycle of a program, project or system. The outcomes of RM, namely sets of validated requirements, are used by many other disciplines as the very basis of their work. These aspects will be discussed in more detail in the following two chapters on the contexts of SE and P&PM.

2

RM from a Systems Engineering Perspective

Chapter Summary

This chapter puts RM into the context of Systems Engineering (SE), defining what is understood by the term 'System' and by the SE approach, as well as explaining why SE is important and what role RM plays in the context of SE.

What is a System?

A system can be defined as an integrated set of interacting elements, such as products, services, people, processes, hardware, software, firmware and information. A system serves a defined purpose. Traditionally, many industries focused on developing products or perhaps services, but taking a system's view bears the great advantage that these products or services can be considered in their operational and industrial contexts, which is arguably more realistic and leads to a more comprehensive approach for their development, integration, marketing and life cycle support.

For example, an aircraft could be seen as a product, but this would be a very simplistic view. Rather, it should be seen as a complex system of integrated subsystems, that is, the aircraft itself, including its maintenance system, its industrial system needed to produce and market the aircraft, the associated training system, and so on.

Also, such a system would be developed in order to be integrated into a 'served' or 'external' system like, for example, the aviation system. An aircraft like the Airbus A380 is a prime example of a highly complex system (Figure 2.1).

Figure 2.1   **The Airbus A380 (Photo: Airbus)**

The concept of the 'served' system versus the 'serving' system has proven very helpful when developing system requirements. Using this concept is particularly popular in the software engineering context where it originated, but it applies at any system level. Figure 2.2 provides a more detailed example of this concept, using an aircraft system as the 'serving' system and the aviation or air transportation system as the 'served' system.

The aviation system can be considered a highly complex 'system of systems'. Some prominent systems within the aviation system are the following: the air traffic control, airport, maintenance, security, catering, disposal, environmental protection, training, airworthiness and certification, travel booking, ground support, spare parts distribution, logistics and transportation, freight and cargo, and passenger systems.

If a company aims to develop an aircraft system that is to operate within the aviation system, the aircraft system would have to interface with or integrate into all relevant systems of the 'served system'.

In some cases, specific component systems of the 'served' system would even have to adapt to the serving system. For example, airport systems had to change due to the sheer size and capacity of the A380 aircraft; that is, new ways to embark and disembark the high number of passengers per flight had to be developed, and runways and aprons enlarged to accommodate for the size and weight of the aircraft.

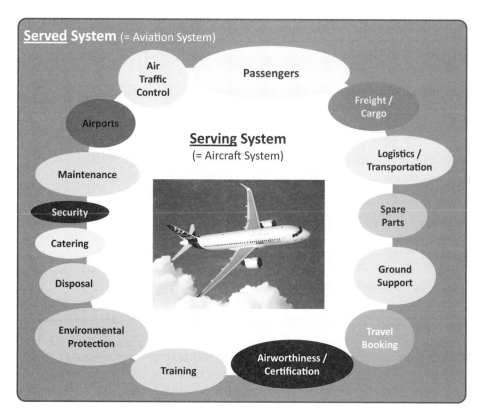

Figure 2.2   The served system and the serving system (Photo: Airbus)

What is Systems Engineering?

Systems Engineering (SE) is an interdisciplinary approach to develop systems. It can be understood to comprise a set of distinctive concepts, methodologies, organizational structures, and so on, that are developed to meet the challenges of engineering highly complex systems, and it entails a number of technical disciplines such as Requirements Management, Design, Manufacturing, Validation and Verification, and Configuration Management that enable the systematic development of such highly complex systems. The processes of these disciplines, and the information that is created and communicated as part of these, need to be maintained over the entire life cycle of a system, and have to be interfaced, integrated and made traceable via SE.

What has become ever more crucial in SE is the understanding of the dynamic interactions and unintended side effects of a system of integrated subsystems. Emerging properties of the integrated system may represent potential opportunities or may turn the integration process into a serious challenge, depending on whether or not these properties are desirable. In any case, these dynamic interactions and side effects need to be proactively managed under SE.

We will now look in more detail at some aspects of SE, including the main disciplines that play a role in SE, and some of their interdependencies. Manufacturing as a discipline is not explicitly addressed here in detail, as the manufactured products or components are usually based on the specified design, which in turn is intended to satisfy the underlying requirements.

MODELING

Modeling plays an increasingly important role within SE. Models are simplified representations of complex reality, designed to support technical activities such as requirements elicitation, analysis and validation, design activities including design verification, product integration and verification, product validation, as well as training and marketing, just to name some important examples. There are many different kinds of models, which are used all over the place, and at all different development levels throughout the extended enterprise.

It is worth keeping in mind, however, that all models are inherently 'wrong' or at least inaccurate to some extent, since they only represent limited aspects of reality that are of interest in a given situation; they aim to be useful for a specific task or research topic at hand. Care must be taken to use models where it makes sense, and always keep in mind their particular limitations.

For example, in software engineering 'prototyping' is good modeling practice to find out about requirements, help express requirements, verify design, integrate software solutions and verify them against the requirements. There are two basic types of such prototypes: those that are only used for a limited purpose during the development – so-called 'throw away' prototypes – and those that are actually extended and completed during the development, until they become part of the final solution.

DESIGN

Design in the context of SE is the discipline that is concerned with finding existing or generating new solutions to satisfy the established system requirements, usually within a given project or program. Design covers many activities from early concept development and selection, via the detailed specification of solution architecture and its intended production and assembly, to the integration of subsystem components into the overall system.

VALIDATION AND VERIFICATION

Validation and Verification (V&V) is an overlapping discipline that covers requirements validation, design verification, product verification, and product validation – although requirements validation is an integral part of the requirements development process, and design verification should be part of the design process.

V&V aims to ensure that (1) the requirements are sufficiently correct, complete and consistent based on the identified stakeholder needs (of both external and internal stakeholders), (2) the system design satisfies the requirements, (3) the product or system satisfies both the requirements and the design, and (4) the final system – once placed into its intended operational context – actually meets the identified customer needs. V&V helps to reduce development risks and the need for corrective rework.

NON-COMPLIANCE AND NON-CONFORMANCE MANAGEMENT

Non-Compliance and Non-Conformance Management (NCM) in the context of SE is the discipline that is concerned with the systematic management of non-compliances and non-conformances. A non-compliance is when a design solution does not comply with the underlying requirements. It is usually identified during the design verification activities and will lead either to a change of the design solution, or the requirements, or alternatively to an accepted deviation that possibly leads to a limitation of the product or system later on.

A non-conformance is when a product or system does not conform with the underlying requirements and/or the design. It is usually identified during the product verification activities, or in some cases during the operational life of a system. It will result either in a necessary change of the product or system, or alternatively a concession and/or a limitation. Any deviations, concessions and limitations will have to be agreed with the relevant stakeholders, including the external customer if the final system is concerned.

CONFIGURATION MANAGEMENT

Configuration Management (CM) is the discipline that focuses on establishing and maintaining consistency of a product or system by ensuring that all related items and their components, as well as any changes to these over time, are known, documented, controlled and tracked.

The traditional scope of CM in the context of SE is often limited, in particular during the early phases of the development process, and regarding the scope of the development data that is managed under CM. This is due to a number of factors such as high volatility of development data in early program phases, high complexity of systems leading to enormous volumes of technical data that have to be managed, high complexity of the extended enterprise that is involved in the development and production of systems, and limited availability of industrially mature methods and tools that enable CM in a way that is sufficiently flexible and that are at the same time capable to manage these ever increasing data volumes.

Being able to conceive a brilliant idea that will reshape the world, and develop that idea into an affordable product or system is one thing. However, it is quite another having the ability to know how you managed to design, produce, manufacture, distribute, operate, maintain, support, modify, phase-out and finally dispose of this product or system. Yet this knowledge is vital if you intend to make more than one such product or system. CM concerns everybody involved in developing, producing, delivering and operating a given product or system along the entire life cycle of that product or system.

Also, CM can be argued to be a prerequisite for increased levels of reuse of requirements, together with existing design solutions that have already been verified against those previously validated requirements.

However, due to its formal character, CM has often been perceived to be a burden to the creative aspects of early development work. Therefore, it is crucial to find the right degree of formality required depending on the stage of the development process. In light of ever shorter 'times to market' with increasing product complexity, the application of lean, agile and dynamic CM becomes mandatory.

In particular during the early development phases, CM must be sufficiently 'light' to allow for frequent, sometimes revolutionary changes or updates of the development items such as user needs, strategies, high-level objectives, and top level requirements. At the same time, the right level of development information needs to be recorded in order to establish traceability, which enables reuse of those items. For instance, if strategy decisions or high-level requirements are changed following a user focus group workshop, those changes and their justification have to be recorded.

The SE participants required to elicit the customer needs and requirements will be the same people as the CM participants for a given system. Product- or system-related data from those many different domains and disciplines will be essential to the SE process, and within this process subject to CM activities. As the project matures and the volume of data increases, the core CM activities of 'identification', 'change management', 'status accounting' and 'audit' can be put under strain, especially if large amounts of corrective action are experienced.

Without requirements there is 'nothing to do'. Without well configured requirements we will have a lot more to do than we think. Many studies in recent years have shown that getting the requirements right and keeping them aligned with changing customer needs over time is crucial for any successful completion of a project or program [10].

However, every attempt to keep changes under control without having traceability in place – at the very least between requirements, design and product baselines – is a big challenge. And this will most likely result in a lot of unnecessary corrective rework, leading to unplanned budget and schedule impacts.

MANAGING SE DATA

Figure 2.3 provides a simplistic overview of a typical 'as is' situation that can be found in many companies today. The 'design' data of a company's products or systems and the corresponding 'product' data may well be under CM (shown by the grey boxes around the design and product data boxes), and are likely to be linked in some formal way from the product back to the corresponding design. This way, it can be easily traced, which version of a given product is based on which version of the corresponding design solution, for example, in terms of drawings or models.

However, the underlying requirements that are to be satisfied by both the design and the product may not be formally specified, or may be of poor quality in terms of correctness, completeness and consistency. Also, there may not be direct links from a given design solution to the correct version of the relevant requirements so that traceability between the requirements and the design may not be immediately available and maintained over time.

Often in such situations, when there are design updates, the relevant requirements are not necessarily revisited to ensure that the update not only meets any new requirements, but also still meets the previous requirements. A lot of corrective rework may be caused by this, when non-compliances emerge later on in the product development process.

Finally, the underlying domain knowledge that influenced the development of requirements as well as the design and the product itself may only be in the heads of individual employees of the company. In other words, this essential domain knowledge is likely not to be specified in a formal and systematic way, so that it is not available for reuse regarding modifications and new developments.

In contrast, Figure 2.4 displays a situation where the available relevant domain knowledge has been elicited and formalized, and is actually used and reused to develop requirements, design solutions and products. This is only reasonably possible if some of the key pieces of information or domain knowledge that are captured, as well as the resulting requirements, are under

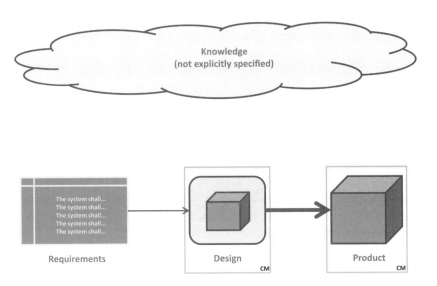

Figure 2.3   Managing SE data – a typical 'as is' situation

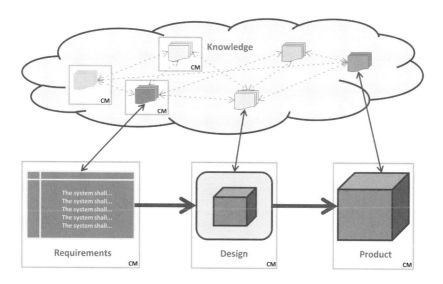

Figure 2.4   Managing SE data – enhancing reuse of domain knowledge

CM as well, not just the design solutions and the product itself. Industrialization aspects and operational feedback loops such as from in-service support will also have to be included in the maintenance of this specified domain knowledge.

Ever more SE related information has to be captured and maintained under CM in order to be able to reuse this information systematically and reliably. The scope of domain knowledge that has to be considered is very large, and not only the product aspects, but also all related industrialization aspects during the entire product or system life cycle have to be managed. This represents a major challenge, since the expected SE data volumes will be of a very different order of magnitude compared to the data volumes that are managed today.

In the majority of cases of complex system development projects or programs, many such domains at different levels of development have to be considered. The SE data produced at each level will have to be linked to corresponding input and output data from other levels within the extended enterprise or the supply network. Figure 2.5 shows how two development levels can be linked in terms of their managed SE data.

Figure 2.6 shows a simplified, yet more integrative view of the development 'V' cycle across three levels of development, in this example the system level, the subsystem level and the component level. In order to keep it simple, the

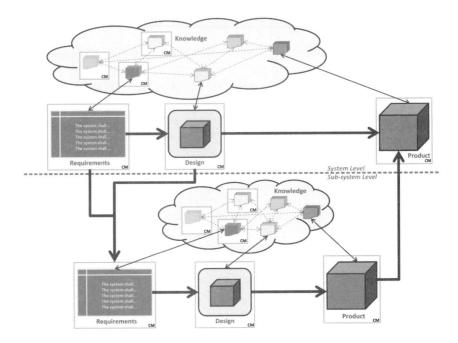

Figure 2.5   Managing SE data – combining two development levels

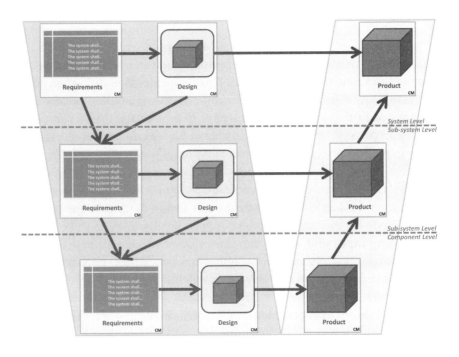

Figure 2.6   Managing SE data – multiple development levels

figure does not show the specified domain knowledge at each level, nor the relevant V&V data, but merely displays the basic types of development data that have to be under CM, namely requirements data, design solution data and product data, as well as the associated traceability information.

What makes this development 'V' cycle very complex is the fact that the real-life development process often does not take place within one company alone at one physical location, but it takes place within a global user network in the context of the extended enterprise, including risk sharing partners, suppliers and subcontractors.

This means that different parts of the development at any level are likely to be in the hands of different organizations that may be separated by cultural, national, language and time zone barriers; yet the development processes and the supporting tooling environments must play together across all these barriers, in particular but not exclusively regarding RM and CM.

Based on the above, Figure 2.7 provides a simplified overview of SE throughout the entire life cycle of a system. The difference can be made between the development life cycle from initial market analyses and project or program conceptions to the delivery and entry into service of a system; and the operational life cycle until the disposal of the system.

The entire life cycle of a system consists of both the development and the operational life cycles, and can span from several months to hundreds of years depending on the system. Usually, during the operational life cycle, a system will undergo a number of modifications to improve the system in the light of in-service experience and/or changing markets or regulations.

The SE approach taken during the development life cycle consists of the combined application of a number of SE disciplines at multiple levels within a complex, global, extended enterprise consisting of risk sharing partners, suppliers and subcontractors.

For later modifications of the system during the operational life cycle, this pattern will be repeated, although usually at a much smaller scope, depending on the nature of each modification in terms of the concerned domains, development levels, and timeframes.

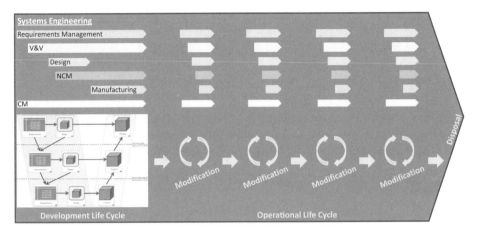

Figure 2.7   A simplified overview of Systems Engineering

Why is SE Important?

SE is important because it helps to make the SE disciplines that were explained above 'play together' in the most effective and efficient manner, in order to develop and deliver systems that satisfy the identified stakeholder needs, at the right level of quality, on time, and within budget.

There is strong evidence that requirements related issues are at the heart of the majority of project failures, delays, or budget overruns [10]. The latter two are often associated with high levels of corrective rework. Yet RM frequently does not seem to be sufficiently interfaced or integrated with other SE disciplines such as design, V&V, NCM, manufacturing, and CM – with CM being widely accepted as the key discipline to ensure traceability, and enable controlled baseline evolutions or iterations throughout the development process. However, the traditional scope of CM in the context of SE is often still limited, in particular in the early phases of the development process, and regarding the scope of the development data that is managed under CM.

Minimizing any requirements related problems is a prerequisite for successful development projects as this will internally reduce the amount of corrective rework. By reducing corrective rework, in turn, companies are likely to achieve quicker 'times to market' and higher profit margins, which allows them to offer lower prices to customers. Also, if the market declines, these companies are in the best position to maintain their market share. It is possible that they may even be able to increase their market share by reducing their prices below those of competitors, and still make a profit where the latter cannot.

This role of SE in ensuring the coordinated and integrated application of the above disciplines becomes ever more essential, since the complexity of systems is increasing at dramatic pace. The following paragraphs will discuss some typical examples of factors that are driving this increase in system complexity, and add pressure to deliver systems ever faster and cheaper.

MARKET AND TECHNOLOGY TRENDS

There are significant, socioeconomic and technological trends, as well as developments of customer expectations, that we should briefly address here in order to enable the successful exploitation of new opportunities, and prevent being taken by surprise. In the following paragraphs, frequent use is made of examples taken from the aviation industry because many readers will be familiar with this industry, at least to a certain extent. However, the points made do of course apply to many industries and markets.

Global, volatile, complex business environments

We are living in a highly globalized market where small events or changes in one market segment of one industry in one part of the world can potentially have immediate and unexpected impacts on seemingly unconnected market segments of apparently unrelated industries around the globe.

Diseases such as the recent outbreaks of bird flu, political uprisings like those during the 'Arab Spring', changed regulations, trading crises and economic recessions, terrorist attacks, wars, natural disasters and many other things do happen and may have dramatic and sudden impacts on even well-established business environments.

All of the above may have a huge impact on how we develop and maintain our products or systems – for instance, by having to introduce new requirements to comply with changed legislation, or by swiftly reacting to changes in market demand with changes in the industrial system. The following are some typical characteristics of these volatile and complex business environments of today.

Increased volatility of markets

Today's markets across most industries seem to be increasingly volatile. Market changes may occur at very high speed, potentially triggered by seemingly unrelated events in other markets across the planet, or natural disasters. Recent examples are the banking crisis and the resulting economic recession all around the world, leading to dramatic declines in sales across many industries.

Although there are some industries with long development cycles and lead times such as the aerospace industry that are less likely to immediately 'feel' the short-term impacts of such changes in the markets, organizations in these industries also need longer to react to relevant changes mainly due to their mere size and complexity. Therefore, it can be argued that they too are experiencing an increased, albeit 'relative' volatility.

Extended enterprises

The notion of the 'extended enterprise' has gained importance as firms become more interconnected, and trade becomes more global. Firms may be connected by contract, as in partnerships, alliances or trade agreements. These alliances, although extremely beneficial, may require changes in processes and related responsibilities. The need to protect intellectual property rights may result in changes; for example, cost repercussions and new proposed designs may require restricted distribution. Time zones can also have significant impacts on the dynamic of information flows and supporting IT tool environments. If all of these issues are well understood and appropriately taken into consideration, the extended enterprise as a network of firms can be extremely beneficial.

Risk sharing partners

Business partnerships in which development costs and consequential benefits are distributed amongst all participating partners can be called 'risk sharing' partnerships. Those involved rely on the commercial success of the business, or of specific projects or programs to receive part of the financial profits from the shared enterprise, while also reducing the risk of loss involved, in case the shared enterprise incurs losses.

Off-shore involvement

Increasingly, customers across many industries expect parts of development programs to be contracted out to companies that are located in specific countries. Often customers will simply not sign their contracts if these expectations are not met in some way or another. Alternatively, companies may not be pushed, but rather choose by themselves to offer significant off-shore involvements in order to increase their chances of winning bids by making a more attractive offer to relevant potential customers. For example, Airbus aircraft are dominating the Chinese market and Airbus has established a Final Assembly Line (FAL) for the A320 family in China.

EVER INCREASING CUSTOMER EXPECTATIONS

Customers have the 'inconvenient' tendency to get used to improved levels of product quality and service quality. For example, some time ago a noisy aircraft without in-flight entertainment may have been the accepted norm for many airlines, and consequently these airlines would have been happy to buy an available standard aircraft that meets their range, payload and safety requirements.

But those days have long gone. Every airline nowadays wishes to see their aircraft highly unique and customized, in line with their own business strategy to satisfy the increasing passenger demands better, and in a more impressive way, than the same aircraft operated by their competitors. As well as supporting their individual branding or business model, they expect their aircraft to work without any technical problems and at operational reliability levels nobody would have ever dared dreaming about 20 years ago.

The following are some typical example areas of increasing customer expectations that are likely to have huge impacts on the current practice of SE, in particular regarding RM and CM because the scope of the information that has to be dealt with by both disciplines will simply be much larger, while response times will have to decrease.

Increased levels of customization

Customers such as airlines do expect ever higher levels of customization of their products and services, since they wish to distinguish themselves from competitors and/or they do not want to change their own business processes more than necessary due to the introduction of a new product or service.

For example, Airbus uses a so-called 'customer definition center' including dedicated lounge areas, showrooms, and conference rooms located close to Cabin Engineering and A350 XWB production. In this center, customers are offered increased levels of flexibility regarding the customization of their cabin layouts and equipment. Customers have the choice from a large variety of 'packages of solutions' that have been developed in close cooperation with customers and suppliers, plus the opportunity to experiment with new, virtual designs.

Increased levels of flexible customer involvement

Increasing numbers of customers wish to be more and more involved in the development or manufacturing of their products. This may be so for a number of reasons ranging from risk reduction, early familiarization of key customer personnel with the product, improved relations at working level with the relevant experts on both the customer side and the supplier side, and finding justifications for concessions that will lead to financial benefits for the customer.

For instance, many airlines send a delegation of technical experts and representatives to the aircraft manufacturing facilities where they can closely monitor the assembly work until the final delivery of a new aircraft.

Reduced development and delivery times

Customers want – and actually need – to be flexible and able to react increasingly swiftly to changes in their markets. In aerospace, both development times of new aircraft and delivery times of already developed aircraft are expected to be ever shorter, so that if the need for a new product is identified by an airline, this need can be satisfied as quickly as possible.

On the other hand, if an aircraft manufacturer is able to develop new products and related services faster than competitors, or offer shorter delivery lead times for existing aircraft to airlines, the manufacturer is likely to be selected – all other product or service characteristics being equal.

Increased reliability

Naturally, customers expect products or services they buy to work as advertised. For example, airlines tend to have very tight schedules of their operations in order to maximize the utilization of their aircraft. If an aircraft has to be grounded for some technical reasons, this potentially causes financial damage to the airline's operation, not to mention the potential loss of passenger satisfaction. Therefore, airlines demand and expect ever higher levels of operational reliability of the aircraft they purchase from aircraft manufacturers.

Reduced times for fixes

Customers increasingly expect immediate fixes to any emerging issues. In the aviation industry, airlines sometimes encounter technical problems which could lead to an aircraft being grounded. In such cases it is imperative that sound technical fixes are developed and deployed very quickly – and without creating any new problems.

Reduced costs

Reducing costs is universally attractive for customers, end-users and suppliers alike. Those companies able to reduce their costs more than their competitors will have an advantage, no matter how they wish to use this advantage. For instance, if an airline has a lower cost basis than their competitors, it may use the lower cost advantage to offer lower fares to passengers, or increase their profit by charging the same fares but at a higher profit margin. Therefore, there are ever increasing expectations to reduce costs. Configured requirements that are linked to verified solutions could be reused by suppliers for other similar products with minimal risk, while helping to reduce costs considerably.

SE, and in particular RM and CM, can be of much help regarding the above customer expectations through increased but controlled reuse, reduction of corrective rework and overall reduced development lead times.

ADVANCED TECHNOLOGICAL TRENDS

Regarding the system or product development process, a number of technological trends can be observed that will be addressed in the following paragraphs, for example the establishment of 3-D printing of parts and components, the integration of Commercial Off The-Shelf (COTS) technology, revolutionary approaches to SE, and increased use of modeling and simulation. All of these trends potentially have huge impacts on how we develop and maintain our products, and they challenge the way how SE and in particular RM and CM are often practiced today.

3-D printing of parts and components

3-D printing is bringing about revolutionary ways of how even the most complex and integrated structures can be produced in a small fraction of the time that was traditionally needed to produce them.

For example, the 'Airbike' was produced entirely out of nylon, using a laser-based manufacturing process known as 'Additive Layer Manufacturing' (ALM) [17]. ALM has also been used to produce parts for satellites and aircraft, and it does not only work with nylon but also with other materials such as stainless steel and titanium [18]. Many of the structures that can now be 3-D printed would be very difficult and wasteful to produce by traditional casting, machining and fabrication techniques.

Although not yet able to produce fully functioning organs, 3-D organ tissue printing has enabled the bespoke production of artificial blood vessels or other components needed for bypass operations or similar surgery.

These are promising steps towards future attempts to print working human organs, for example, for patients that are waiting for donated organs but are running out of time. 3-D models of organs can be produced, then tissue from the patient is used to seed a 3-D printer, which creates a new organ layer by layer over the course of several hours. In the future, these printers may also be able to print new skin straight onto patients with burns, or other similar injuries.

There are many examples of 3-D printing applications that are not fully mature yet, such as the production of replacement organs in the medical field or local structural repair in the aerospace and automotive industries. However, it can be expected that in a number of years, 3-D printing will have revolutionized many areas across many industries.

Production lead times and overall costs will be dramatically minimized due to process time reductions and the elimination of material waste, while production flexibility in terms of both customization and product changes over time will be significantly increased. The current practice of SE in the industrial context, in particular regarding RM and CM, may soon be the limiting factor of the development process, and risks to become disconnected because it seems to 'take too long' to do SE.

In other words, the practice of SE and RM (as integral part of it) has to evolve and become leaner, more agile and dynamic in order to keep pace and actually enable the systematic exploitation of these new advances in manufacturing.

Integration of COTS technology

The required integration of COTS technology has significantly added to the complexity in most system development projects or programs. For example, if laptops and display screens form part of a frigate development contract, these COTS items are expected to be up-to-date at delivery. This is a major challenge from a number of viewpoints such as performance, shock and vibration, resilience, security, physical integration, functional integration, and emerging system properties. SE has to enable the systematic functional and non-functional integration of COTS components into the overall system throughout both the development life cycle and the operational life cycle of the system at hand.

Revolutionary approaches to SE

Some scientists believe that the traditional SE processes, some of which have been in use since the pre-Apollo era, are no longer adequate for the large, complex systems that have to be developed in many industries today. Typically, unintended and unanticipated interactions between elements of systems are often only uncovered during integration, testing, or even worse, in service [19].

It is established current practice to segregate a design into separable elements often represented in a 'V' cycle, with evolutions of the design taking place on the down-stroke, and the system integration and verification on the upstroke. Failure usually occurs at the interfaces between system elements thought to be separate. The unintended and unanticipated reactions of systems with other systems often remain unnoticed until late in the development process, and usually result in unplanned rework. Hence, the need arises to minimize unintended consequences as early as possible in the system development process. SE and RM have to reflect this need.

Increased modeling and simulation capabilities

In many industries, modeling and simulation are increasingly used at all steps of the product development process and at all levels of development, for instance in order to analyze and later validate requirements, analyze impacts of changes during the development process, as well as verify design solutions and later the finished product.

Many companies have been developing and using rapid prototyping methods for many years. One example from Airbus that is related to hardware models is the use of rapid prototyping for wind tunnel testing, where three-dimensional stereo lithography machines are used to produce needed components, based on direct metal laser-sintering techniques. Current materials that can be used to produce these prototypes encompass light alloys, steels, super-alloys and standard industrial materials like stainless steel. The scope of SE, in particular of RM and CM, has to be extended to cover these new capabilities, while contributing to reduce overall development times.

What Role Does RM Play in the Context of SE?

Based on the above discussion we can see that RM is one of the key disciplines in the scope of SE, because everything that is developed in the context of a given project or program and that is later modified throughout the entire system life cycle must be based on validated requirements.

RM can be called the 'cornerstone' of SE because it is the discipline concerned with pointing into the overall direction of all technical efforts. Everything that is not required will not even be attempted to be achieved; and everything that is required has to be achieved, or at least it needs to be known that something is required but cannot be achieved for some reason, so that the situation can be dealt with in the light of this knowledge.

Looking at the overall SE context, requirements have to be developed and managed over time at every level of development, in every engineering team or work package, and every effort to design, manufacture, assemble, integrate, verify and validate will be based on these requirements. If the requirements are of high quality in terms of correctness, completeness and consistency, we stand a good chance of developing the right system in the right way, within schedule and budget. If, however, the requirements are of low quality, we risk developing a system that does not satisfy the needs of the stakeholders, is too expensive, and takes too much time to develop.

Design, therefore, needs 'good' requirements because this discipline is concerned with identifying existing or creating new solutions that satisfy the applicable requirements. If the requirements are wrong, the design will be wrong.

If the requirements are correct but no design solution can be found because the needed technology is not available yet, or because there are other technical conflicts that cannot be solved yet, this information is very important to know as well.

Traditionally in such cases, requirements were often made 'softer' or less demanding so that the available solution would then satisfy them. This, however, is a dangerous thing to do. It is better to know that certain correct requirements cannot currently be met, and to manage this situation proactively. NCM is the discipline concerned with such cases, and systematically addresses and manages them.

Regarding V&V, requirements are validated to be of good quality in terms of correctness, completeness and consistency, design solutions are verified against the applicable requirements which the design aims to satisfy, and later on the system is verified against the underlying system requirements and the system design including assembly aspects, which is also based on the system requirements. All V&V activities are directly or indirectly based on requirements.

Finally, CM focuses on establishing and maintaining the consistency of a system by ensuring that all related items and their components, as well as any changes to these over time, are known, documented, controlled and tracked. All such items and components and their changes over time are directly or indirectly based on requirements, and subsequent changes of requirements. Hence, it is safe to state that RM is crucial to SE.

3

RM from a Project and Program Management Perspective

Chapter Summary

This chapter puts RM into the context of Project and Program Management (P&PM), explaining the difference between projects and programs, defining the discipline of P&PM, as well as explaining why this discipline is important and what role RM plays in the context of P&PM.

What is a Project?

A project is a unique and temporary process consisting of a set of coordinated and controlled workflows and related activities with a specific duration, as well as explicit start and finish dates. A project is undertaken to achieve a set of unique objectives, although the final outcome of how these objectives will be met are likely not to be known exactly from the outset of a project. Each project will be subject to a set of requirements that often will have to be developed as part of the project, as well as a number of other constraints such as budget, schedule and resource availability.

Projects may be categorized into system development or modification projects, business improvement projects, information system/information technology (IS/IT) projects, and research and technology (R&T) projects.

For example, a car manufacturer may decide to develop a new version of an existing type of car that has an all-electric engine. This development could be managed as a project within the overall program that manages the existing type of car including the new electric version.

What is a Program?

A program intends to deliver a specific business case, which usually includes revenues from external sources and profit to the company. It spans across the total life cycle of a system or product, and coordinates a set of technical, administrative and financial tasks that are intended to develop, produce and support a system for the benefit of the stakeholders. It consists of a set of related or embedded projects and recurring processes. A program is managed in a coordinated way in order to obtain business benefits and control that would otherwise not be achievable by merely managing the related projects in isolation.

For instance, a national government may run a secondary education development program that is partly financed by the United Nations and a number of individual member countries. Within the program there are likely to be a number of projects that manage certain aspects of the program such as specific school construction projects, a national curriculum project, and a project that aims to increase the percentage of girls that attend secondary education.

What is Project and Program Management?

Project and Program Management (P&PM) is the discipline concerned with the management of projects and programs in the context of SE. Project Management includes requirements management, project establishment, monitoring and control, schedule management, cost management, material resource management, risk and opportunity management, supplier management, project closure and handover, as well as human resource management.

In addition to that, Program Management has to define and implement business strategy, and steer a set of related or embedded projects and recurring processes during the entire life cycle of a system, with the aim to generate some stakeholder benefits such as profit.

For each project, the following phases can be identified:

1.   The 'Feasibility Phase' aims to establish the project viability and provide all the useful and relevant information before deciding if the project can be launched.

2.   The 'Planning Phase' aims to define and refine objectives. It is also the time to select and plan out the best alternative courses of action to reach these objectives.

3.   The 'Executing and Controlling Phase' aims to coordinate the resources needed to carry out the plan and to ensure that project objectives will be met.

4.   The 'Closing Phase' aims to formalize acceptance of the project, bring it to an orderly end, appraise its performance and finalize the capture of experience.

Apart from RM, which was already introduced in the first chapter, we will now look in turn to the following activities that are part of P&PM: schedule management, material resource management, human resource management, cost management, supplier management, monitoring and control, earned value management, and risk and opportunity management.

SCHEDULE MANAGEMENT

Schedule Management in the context of P&PM is the discipline concerned with planning all identified work activities throughout the project or program. The discipline is closely linked to the work breakdown structure of the project or program.

Figure 3.1 provides an example project schedule for a typical business improvement project. The screenshot only shows the high-level phases and their duration with project milestones. For each phase, detailed and often interdependent activities are listed (not shown here) that have to be carried out in order to achieve the corresponding project milestones. Each such activity or milestone has to be managed in detail in the project schedule. For example, changes to the availability of needed resources for specific activities and their progress made have to be kept up to date in the schedule, so that any knock-on effects can be identified.

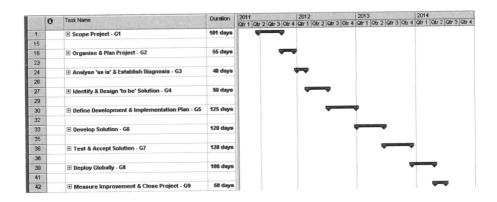

	0	Task Name	Duration	2011				2012				2013				2014			
				Qtr 1	Qtr 2	Qtr 3	Qtr 4	Qtr 1	Qtr 2	Qtr 3	Qtr 4	Qtr 1	Qtr 2	Qtr 3	Qtr 4	Qtr 1	Qtr 2	Qtr 3	Qtr 4
1		⊞ Scope Project - G1	101 days																
15																			
16		⊞ Organise & Plan Project - G2	55 days																
23																			
24		⊞ Analyse 'as is' & Establish Diagnosis - G3	40 days																
26																			
27		⊞ Identify & Design 'to be' Solution - G4	90 days																
29																			
30		⊞ Define Development & Implementation Plan - G5	125 days																
32																			
33		⊞ Develop Solution - G6	120 days																
35																			
36		⊞ Test & Accept Solution - G7	120 days																
38																			
39		⊞ Deploy Globally - G8	100 days																
41																			
42		⊞ Measure Improvement & Close Project - G9	50 days																

Figure 3.1   An example project schedule (Business Improvement Project)

MATERIAL RESOURCE MANAGEMENT

Material Resource Management in the context of P&PM is the discipline concerned with planning and putting in place the material resources needed for the successful completion of a project or program. This discipline is closely linked to the system or product breakdown structure, the work breakdown structure, and the schedule of the project or program.

HUMAN RESOURCE MANAGEMENT

Human Resource Management in the context of P&PM is the discipline concerned with planning and controlling the availability of the human resources needed in order to successfully carry out a project or program. This discipline is closely linked to the work breakdown structure and schedule of the project or program.

COST MANAGEMENT

Cost Management in the context of P&PM is the discipline concerned with planning, controlling and forecasting the recurring and non-recurring costs of a project or program. Cost management is closely linked with the system or product breakdown structure and the related work breakdown structure. The discipline covers the areas of financial accounting and management accounting for the project or program at hand.

Figure 3.2 provides an example cash flow table and associated chart for a typical system development project. The table includes cash inflows such as customer payments following project milestones, and cash outflows such as for working hours and facilities paid. Such tables and charts help to control the cash flow of a project or program.

Earned value management (EVM) is closely related to cost management and is often taken to be part of it; although EVM is also concerned with schedule management. Whether it is included in cost management or not, EVM helps with forecasting the total cost at the completion of a project, in the light of the progress made at a given point in time during the project.

	2012											
	Jan	Feb	Mar	Apr	May	Jun	Jul	Aug	Sep	Oct	Nov	Dec
Cash at 1st of month	197	42	-53	367	272	152	32	-45	-140	110	65	15
Inflow												
Customer payments	0	0	570	0	0	0	0	0	400	0	0	0
Tax return	0	0	0	0	0	0	43	0	0	0	0	0
RSP participations	0	25	0	25	0	0	0	25	0	25	0	0
Total inflow	0	25	570	25	0	0	43	25	400	25	0	0
Outflow												
Working hours	90	90	110	90	90	90	90	90	110	60	40	20
Facilities	30	30	30	30	30	30	30	30	30	10	10	10
Assets	28	0	0	0	0	0	0	0	0	0	0	0
Licences	7	0	0	0	0	0	0	0	0	0	0	0
Ext services	0	0	10	0	0	0	0	0	10	0	0	0
Total outflow	155	120	150	120	120	120	120	120	150	70	50	30
Cash at end of month	42	-53	367	272	152	32	-45	-140	110	65	15	-15

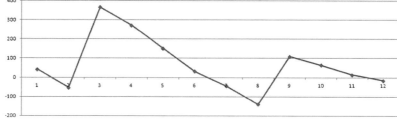

Figure 3.2   An example cash flow table and chart (System Development Project)

RISK AND OPPORTUNITY MANAGEMENT

Risk and Opportunity Management in the context of P&PM is the discipline concerned with identifying, categorizing, prioritizing, mitigating (where appropriate for risks), exploiting (where appropriate for opportunities), and tracking any identified risks or opportunities that are relevant for a given project or program.

Figure 3.3 provides an example risk register for an IS/IT project. Major risks of an RM tool update project are identified. For each such risk, the main root causes are elaborated that are likely to cause the risk to become a real issue or problem. These identified root causes are directly addressed by a number of suitable mitigation actions in order to eliminate or at least reduce the impact of the root causes, and thereby reduce the associated risks.

SUPPLIER MANAGEMENT

Supplier Management in the context of P&PM is the discipline concerned with planning and managing all non-technical aspects of subcontracting work packages within the extended enterprise for a given project or program. This can be very challenging, especially when the extended enterprise consists of risk-sharing partners, suppliers and subcontractors who are geographically dispersed across different nations, cultures and languages.

MONITORING AND CONTROL

Monitoring and Control in the context of P&PM is the discipline concerned with continuously checking progress made against the established project plan, and identifying any actual or potential deviations from it by means of relevant Key Performance Indicators (KPIs). The main purpose of this discipline is to highlight emerging risks and issues; and signal when corrective actions are necessary.

EARNED VALUE MANAGEMENT

Earned Value (EV) is the value of work that was performed for a component of the work breakdown structure (WBS) of a project in a specific period of time.

EV is usually contrasted with the Planned Value (PV) of the work that was planned to be performed for the same component of the WBS in the same period of time. EV may also be contrasted to the Actual Cost (AC) incurred for the work performed for the component of the WBS in question, in the same period of time.

EVM is a project management technique that enables ongoing tracking of the project progress made in terms of EV as opposed to the planned progress, or the AC incurred – all for the same work for a given component of the WBS

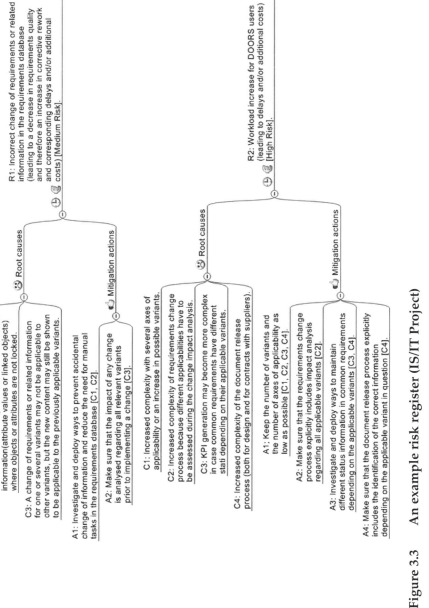

Figure 3.3   An example risk register (IS/IT Project)

in a specific period of time. EV may be tracked on a weekly or monthly basis, or at important milestones of a given project.

The identified cost incurred and time spent for progress achievement can be compared with the planning. This enables a decision on corrective actions in the short term, and make predictions for cost controlling purposes. For example, the total project cost at completion can be predicted using this approach for the entire project.

Figure 3.4 provides an example EVM chart that shows the EV, PV and AC curves of a given WBS component of a project. You should first look at the EV curve and compare it with (1) the PV curve in order to assess the schedule performance; and (2) with the AC curve to assess the cost performance. Regarding the former, only PV and EV data points should be compared that correspond to the same percentage of completion of a given WBS component.

Figure 3.5 provides a simplified overview of P&PM throughout the entire life cycle of a system. Similar to Figure 2.7 that gave an overview of SE throughout the life cycle of a system, Figure 3.5 shows in the lower part the development and operational life cycles of a system until its disposal, with a number of modifications throughout its operational life cycle.

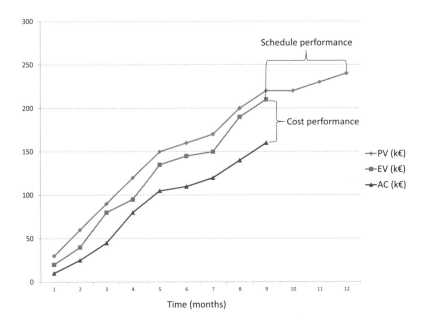

Figure 3.4   An example Earned Value Management chart

Program Management covers the entire life cycle of this system. Although not shown in much detail here, all P&PM disciplines that were previously described have to be covered during the entire life cycle as part of Program Management. There will naturally be times, where the needed efforts in this domain will be greatest, namely before and during the development of the system at hand, and before and during major modifications of the system over time.

RM is shown here as a continuous activity within Program Management. The requirements that are developed and managed over time in the context of Program Management are mainly requirements that the program itself has to satisfy, as opposed to system requirements that the system has to satisfy.

Project Management covers the development life cycle and every individual modification project life cycle of the system. All P&PM disciplines mentioned above have to be covered during the development project and each subsequent modification project.

RM is shown here as a continuous activity under Project Management. The requirements that are developed and managed in this context are mainly requirements that the project itself has to satisfy within the program, as opposed to the system requirements that the system under development has to satisfy.

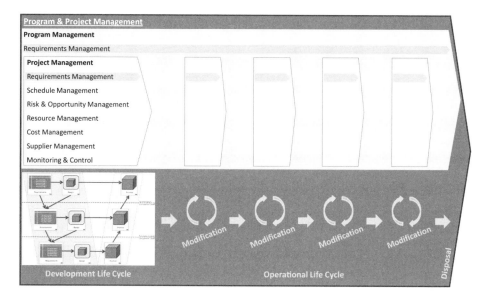

Figure 3.5   A simplified overview of Project and Program Management

For example, if several variants of a system are developed in parallel such as different aircraft family members of a new aircraft family, each of these variants may be developed as an 'independent' project within the overall aircraft family program.

Why is P&PM Important?

Any organization has to be able to cope with changes in its environment and even initiate change proactively in order to survive and grow, while fulfilling its purpose. Change has to be brought about both responsively and proactively in order to address threats and exploit opportunities for the organization.

Projects or programs that comprise a number of projects are usually the means to drive and control significant change in a systematic manner. They are used to get things done that do not normally form part of the day-to-day activities of the organization.

P&PM is the crucial 'umbrella' discipline that enables systematic and successful change, driven and controlled within and by organizations. The main concerns of P&PM are to systematically achieve specific targets of an organization by planning, establishing, controlling and completing programs and projects – within agreed schedules and budgets, and delivering at the right quality. Hence P&PM is key to any organization's very future.

What Role Does RM Play in the Context of P&PM?

In profit-oriented organizations, projects or programs are only run if the company expects to make a profit by doing so, in one way or another. In not-for-profit organizations, projects or programs are only run if they are affordable in terms of time and budget, and actually provide the needed benefits.

The generic objectives for any kind of project or program are to (1) provide customers, clients or other stakeholders with something they need (that is, the system to be delivered) that has to actually help them to improve how they do things now (without the new system), (2) at the right quality and price (because they need to be satisfied or even delighted) and (3) when they need it, that is, at the agreed delivery date.

This is constrained by what the customers, clients or other stakeholders can afford, in other words by what can be delivered in the mutual interest. The customer pays for the delivered system, yet in many cases he does not use the system himself, but benefits from other people using it.

Customer needs are usually not what customers say they want. Therefore, the real needs should be established jointly, based on what customers think they want as a starting point. If customers are not successful with the new system, they will not be able to pay for it. And if they are not more successful with the new system than they are without it, they will not want to pay for the new system.

For a project or program, the requirements are what the project or program is planning to satisfy. Both sides, that is, the customer and the organization that runs the program or project should benefit from it. If the system requirements are not of good quality (in the sense of being correct, complete and consistent), time will be spent on doing the wrong things. All supporting P&PM activities will be wasted.

Furthermore, it is not only important that the right system is developed and delivered, but also that the system is developed and delivered in the right way. Whereas the former would be reflected in the system requirements, the latter would be reflected in the program or project requirements, and probably in the requirements of the enabling system such as the industrial system that needs to be developed in order to produce and deliver the new system.

Schedule Management is based on the system breakdown structure and the corresponding WBS, which in turn is based on what needs to be achieved, that is, the requirements. If the requirements are wrong, the schedule is wrong.

Material Resource Management is based on the system breakdown structure and the program or project schedule, both of which are based on the requirements. If the requirements are wrong, we will not get what we need, when we need it.

Human Resource Management, again, is based on the system breakdown structure, the corresponding WBS, and the program or project schedule, which in turn are based on what needs to be achieved, that is, the requirements. If the requirements are wrong, the program or project probably does not to have the right resources with the right skills and experience in place, when needed.

Cost Management is based on the system breakdown structure (recurring costs), WBS (non-recurring costs) and the corresponding program or project schedule (timing of costs incurred), all of which are based on the requirements. If the requirements are wrong, the overall development costs will be much higher due to corrective rework, as a direct result of which the schedule will be wrong and the program or project cash flow will be out of control.

Supplier Management serves to manage the risk-sharing partners, suppliers, and subcontractors within the extended enterprise, in order to make sure that needed subsystems will be delivered by them as contractually agreed at the right quality, price and time. All of this is subject to the requirements that were signed as part of the contract. If the requirements are wrong, the wrong system may be delivered at the wrong time and for the wrong price, probably leading to substantial additional costs and delays that will be caused by the necessary corrective rework.

Monitoring and Control is about making sure we get where we want to be, taking the way we have agreed, which is all specified in the program or project requirements and the system requirements. If the requirements are wrong, we are monitoring and controlling our way to somewhere we do not want to be, taking a path we do not want to take.

Risk and Opportunity Management needs to be closely linked to RM. Risks are often based on specific assumptions, on which certain requirements are based. Also, opportunities may lead to the development of new requirements or the modification of existing requirements. If the requirements are not properly linked to risks and opportunities, any efforts to manage risks and opportunities may soon be disconnected from reality in terms of the program, project or system requirements that drive the overall activities of the program or project.

As mentioned before, there is strong evidence that requirements-related issues are at the heart of the majority of project failures, delays or budget overruns. Since the latter two are usually associated with high levels of corrective rework, minimizing any requirements-related problems is a prerequisite for successful development projects, as this will significantly contribute to reduce the amount of corrective rework.

To summarize, RM plays a crucial role not only in the context of SE but also in both Program and Project Management throughout the entire life cycle of a system.

PART II

Putting Requirements Management into Practice

4

Human Factors – The Key to Success

Chapter Summary

This chapter will look in detail at some of the key human aspects that need addressing when implementing or running any complex business process in general, and the proposed RM process in particular, in any organization. We will first answer the question why human factors are so important. Then we will turn to some key communication aspects. Third, essential change management issues will be discussed, in order to minimize harmful frictions, conflicts and resistance when implementing new processes, methods or tools. Fourth, we will look at a number of service related aspects, which need to be kept in mind both when trying to cover service related requirements in any RM approach, and when actually implementing a new RM approach such as the one proposed in this book within a given company. The chapter concludes with a helpful summary of 'dos' and 'don'ts' when putting the proposed RM process into practice in a particular context.

Why Are Human Factors So Important?

Companies are not deterministic machines that reliably follow correct processes, which lead to predictable deliverables at the right quality, time and cost. Sometimes, we might think that we would like companies to be like this, because it would be so much easier to manage our activities in projects and programs. But the reality is very different. Companies are full of highly complex and unique human individuals, with a tremendous range of gifts, skills and experience, different cultural backgrounds, as well as different values and behaviors in life.

Therefore, the real context of any business or organization is not a context of uniform process actors that perfectly and reliably carry out pre-defined process activities in order to deliver the correct process outputs based on the correct process inputs. Rather, it is a highly complex context of very different human beings, with all our faults and weaknesses as such. Depending on our personalities and the day, even the time of the day in question, and what happened to us at home or on our way to work, we might be angry, desperate, fed up, sad, happy, very proud of ourselves or indeed ashamed. We might be in the middle of our mid-life crisis, or in full career development mode.

If we wish to make progress with our program, project or system development, we need to be able to take us and the people around us as we are, exploit our strengths, and live with our weaknesses in the most constructive way possible. We always hear that companies' 'employees are the most important assets'. While this is true, the question may be asked what companies do about it? Unfortunately, in many companies this statement is not much more than a hollow phrase, and employees are put under tremendous negative pressure and stress when they work in project or program teams.

'Drum-beating' exercises are common P&PM practice in many companies. This sounds like a comparison from the era of slavery, and it is actually perceived as such by many employees. It may be preferable to think and talk about P&PM as 'conducting' project work, like a conductor would conduct the concert of a symphonic orchestra.

Employees' motivation is obviously crucial to conducting a program or project successfully. Unmotivated employees can have disastrous effects on any undertaking, even more so if the available budget and time are scarce. Highly motivated employees, on the other hand, are able to achieve the most remarkable things in the most challenging programs and projects such as space missions, the development of an airliner, or the construction of a motorway bridge or a tunnel under the sea.

Assuming that for most employees in affluent and developed societies their basic needs such as for housing, food and protection from harm are satisfied, the things that will motivate people most are that they feel they are taken seriously, valued, trusted, appreciated, empowered, supported, and given the opportunity to build and achieve their own professional career aspirations.

When deploying the RM process, in particular during the first-time deployment, many people in an organization are directly or indirectly concerned. Requirements Managers will have to roll out the process and are likely to face a number of people that will be opposed to this for a variety of reasons. These possible reasons will be discussed in detail later in this chapter. But even when simply applying the deployed RM process, they will have to interact and communicate with relevant stakeholders and domain experts, on whose cooperation they depend in order to develop and maintain their requirements.

Therefore it is of utmost importance to take all the people involved in the RM process seriously, with honest and mutual respect, recognizing and acknowledging them as what they are – unique, complex, precious human beings with many strengths but also faults and weaknesses.

Communication Aspects

Given the nature and importance of human factors in any organization such as companies or project teams, communication aspects are of particular relevance. Communications in the widest possible sense serve to identify all necessary participants in the RM process, to inform them about the process itself and their expected level of involvement or participation, to elicit, capture and discuss the many pieces of information needed for the development of requirements and their maintenance over time, as well as to negotiate and validate requirements with the relevant stakeholders.

Also communications are needed to transmit the necessary Key Performance Indicators (KPIs) regarding the RM process to the people responsible for the ongoing P&PM and SE efforts, in particular for monitoring and controlling activities.

Last but not least, communications are needed to create a positive attitude among all participants in the RM process regarding their own participation. They need to be informed about the progress made, any concerns, fears or discomfort need to be addressed, and positive trust relationships should be established between the Requirements Manager and all his relevant stakeholders and domain experts.

One of the key principles of communication is that it does not matter what we think we have said, but what the recipient of our communication thinks we have said. Hence, we should try to increase the likelihood of our message being correctly understood, and we should actually make sure it has been.

The likelihood of our message being understood can be increased by:

- Finding out what means of communication the recipient prefers, for example, email, telephone, or face-to-face contact, and then using the corresponding communication channels.

- Avoiding the use of RM jargon or abbreviations and expressions that may be foreign to the recipient. Rather we should try to speak the recipient's own language whenever possible. This applies to both the technical language and the actual native language of the recipient.

- Trying to keep our message as short and concise as possible. This will have two impacts: first, the recipient will find it easier to understand what we are saying, and second, the recipient will not be annoyed if he feels that we are trying not to waste his time (most participants in the RM process tend to be very busy).

We can make sure that our message has actually been understood by observing the reactions of the recipient during a face-to-face communication, by asking if we have sufficiently well explained what we wanted to say and by asking the recipient if he is fine with what we have said – while possibly repeating the main message.

It is crucial not to underestimate the importance of communication aspects when dealing with human beings. Of course, the above also applies the other way around for communications from the RM process participant to the Requirements Manager. Hence, when you (in this function) capture information from relevant stakeholders or domain experts, you should make sure that you have understood them correctly.

Change Management Aspects

As any change associated with the implementation of new processes, methods or tools needs to be managed in some form in order to minimize harmful frictions, conflicts and resistance, some essential change management issues are discussed in this section. In doing so, we should first take a brief look at some developments in the general business context, before suggesting a number of strategies of how resistance can be pre-empted and how change can be managed and implemented within organizations.

Many companies have successfully re-engineered their core processes by unifying activities that were previously divided into sub-activities done by different departments, and cutting off activities that do not add value to the overall process. Those companies assign outstanding managers as 'process owners', responsible for optimizing core processes across all traditional functions. They are given the authority to form multifunctional teams and are assigned specific resources to achieve their objectives. In addition to that, new evaluation and reward systems are introduced, as well as new career paths that focus on process management. What really matters to those 'process organizations' is real teamwork and the customer.

It has been argued that 'traditional leadership styles are inappropriate in process organizations. Managers cannot give orders and control; they have to negotiate and cooperate' [20]. Processes should be standardized to a certain extent in order to improve productivity, but still leave the company sufficiently flexible to be able to customize offerings and satisfy differing customer needs [20].

Change in general is not something that a company should try to suppress. On the contrary, change that is carefully managed can be argued to be necessary and beneficial to enable the company to cope with external and internal developments that cannot directly be influenced by the company. Companies need to constantly rethink whether their strategic goals are still in the best interest of the company and if what they are doing is still suitable to reach those strategic goals.

Events such as the 9/11 attacks and market developments like the appearance of low-cost airlines, for instance, mark points or periods in time when change is most urgently needed. Many airlines, airports and also aircraft manufacturers

– usually those that were best able to change – managed to survive and adapt to the new situation, while others went out of business.

But also less dramatic changes such as the implementation of a new RM process with supporting methods and tools, like the RM process that is proposed in this book, are potentially prone to obstacles and resistance. Change management issues need to be addressed to ensure that the advantages of the new process are fully realized.

Major problems during the implementation can be confusion, role conflict and ambiguity, as well as conflict generation among employees, if the implementation is not carefully planned and carried out. Because considerable shifts of power and controllable resources occur in the course of most change implementations, some individuals and groups are likely to be jealous and show resistance to the structural changes. From a corporate culture perspective, change management becomes even more important.

A classic approach to dealing with resistance when implementing change has been offered by Kotter et al. [21]. They identified four reasons for individual resistance to change in organizations:

- parochial self-interest;

- misunderstanding and lack of trust;

- different assessments of the benefits of change;

- low tolerance for change.

They proposed six strategies to deal with resistance, depending on the given circumstances (see Table 4.1). Choices of those strategies have to be 'internally consistent and fit key situational variables'. The latter two strategies of 'manipulation/cooptation' or 'explicit/implicit coercion' should not be used, because long-term employee commitment to the changes is absolutely critical for any company to become a working process organization [21].

Table 4.1   Strategies for dealing with resistance (adapted from Kotter et al., 1986) [21]

Approach	Commonly used where …	Advantages	Drawbacks
(1) Education/ communications	… *lack of information* … *lack of analysis*	+ once persuaded, people will help	– time-consuming
(2) Participation/ involvement	… *initiator needs information* … *others have power to resist*	+ commitment + information and support	– time-consuming
(3) Facilitation/ support	… *resistance due to adjustment problems*	+ works best against problems	– time-consuming – expensive – can still fail
(4) Negotiation/ agreement	… *initiator would lose* … *group powerful resistor*	+ easy way to avoid major resistance	– expensive – subordinate compliance
(5) Manipulation/ cooptation	… *other tactics do not work* … *or are too expensive*	+ quick + inexpensive	– problems if people feel manipulated
(6) Explicit/ implicit coercion	… *speed is essential* … *initiator very powerful*	+ speedy + overcomes any resistance	– risky if people get mad

For most major changes to the way of working in an organization (regarding process, method and tool matters alike) it seems very beneficial to (1) develop local change agents as early as possible; (2) identify and target opinion leaders directly; (3) use existing communication channels, especially informal ones; (4) model and demonstrate what the changes are about in order to convince opinion leaders; (5) use the new way of working in areas, where short-term improvements can be achieved that help to reduce employee uncertainty while delivering quick 'wins'; and (6) develop local experts in order to provide support for the long-term use of the new way of working.

Several alternative implementation strategies are widely used to implement new systems, but they can also be used to implement new processes, methods and tools:

- The big bang strategy, where the ready-made new system is implemented across the whole organization at once. Although duplication of work is saved using this method, it is very risky and represents a very high and sudden workload to employees.

- Parallel running is a lower-risk approach that allows for employees building up confidence with the new system because the old and the new way of doing things are running at the same time. However, this approach is expensive and means a higher workload for employees because there is duplication of work.

- The phased approach represents a useful compromise insofar as it allows for modifications and does not expose the whole company at once if there are still major problems with the new system. Within parts of the company the new system can be integrated by using either of the above approaches, until step by step the new system is implemented in the whole company.

- The pilot study approach seems suitable for high-risk projects, but is time-consuming and expensive.

One very comprehensive and compelling approach to change management has been proposed by Kotter [22] with his 'eight-stage process of creating major change' (see Table 4.2). He argues that most changes suffer from sufficient momentum over time and tend to sink in the 'quicksand of complacency' or provoke serious resistance, because not all eight stages have been covered or only superficially so [22].

Kotter emphasizes that there is a crucial and clear distinction between management and leadership that must be understood in order to avoid misunderstandings about managers' roles in a company, and get the 'right' people to do the matching job in major change processes.

'Management', according to Kotter, means planning, budgeting, organizing, staffing, controlling and problem-solving, and produces a degree of predictability and order. It has the potential to consistently produce the short-term results expected, such as being on time and within budget.

'Leadership', on the other hand, means establishing direction, that is, developing a vision of the future, aligning people, motivating and inspiring. Leadership has the potential to produce extremely useful change, often to a dramatic degree, such as new products that customers want, new organizational structures that are more responsive and focus on core processes as opposed to pure functionality, or new approaches with labor unions that make a firm more competitive in the marketplace.

Leadership creates a vision and strategies to achieve that vision, whereas management creates plans to implement those strategies and budgets to convert those plans into financial projections and goals. This is not to say that a manager should either manage or lead, but rather he may have to do both, depending on the given position and responsibilities. In general, top management should focus more (but not exclusively) on leadership (to give direction), whereas middle and lower management should focus more (but not exclusively) on management (to make it happen). The crucial point here is to use the right mix of resources at each level to provide both good leadership and at the same time sound management within any company [22].

To summarize, it can be said that carefully planned and managed change is more likely to result in the successful implementation of any new way of working. The above offers some advice on what needs to be considered and which approach could be taken in a specific situation, when implementing the RM approach proposed in this book.

Table 4.2   **The eight-stage process of creating major change (adapted from Kotter, 1996) [22]**

(1) Establishing a sense of urgency
• Examining the market and competitive realities • Identifying and discussing crises, potential crises and major opportunities • Fighting complacency (making crises visible, setting higher standards, restructuring parts of the company in a way that widens employees' functional goals and allows for receiving customer contact, avoiding too much 'happy talk' by top management)
(2) Creating the guiding coalition
• Putting together a group with enough power to lead the change (position power, expertise, credibility and leadership, as well as management skills) • Getting the group to work as a team (creating trust and common goals)
(3) Developing a vision and strategy
• Creating an effective vision to help direct the change effort (this vision needs to be imaginable, desirable, feasible, focused, flexible and communicable) • Developing strategies for achieving that vision
(4) Communicating the change vision
• Using every vehicle possible to constantly communicate the new vision and strategies (keep it simple, use verbal pictures and all channels available, especially emphasize dialogue whenever possible, keep repeating the message, lead by example, explain seeming inconsistencies) • Having the guiding coalition role-model the behavior expected of employees

Table 4.2   *Concluded*

(5) Empowering employees for broad-based action
• Getting rid of obstacles (that is barriers to empowerment such as bosses discouraging employees from participating in the change process, formal structures making it more difficult for employees, lack of needed skills, lack of suitable information systems)   • Changing systems or structures that undermine the change vision   • Encouraging risk-taking and non-traditional ideas, activities and actions
(6) Generating short-term wins
• Planning for visible performance improvement (wins)   • Creating those wins   • Visibly recognizing and rewarding the people who made those wins possible
(7) Consolidating change and producing more change
• Using increased credibility to change all systems, structures and policies that do not fit together and do not fit the transformation vision   • Hiring, developing and promoting people who can implement the change vision   • Reinvigorating the process with new projects, themes and change agents
(8) Anchoring new approaches in the culture
• Creating better performance through customer- and productivity-oriented behavior, more and better leadership, and more effective management   • Articulating the connections between new behaviors and organizational success   • Developing means to ensure leadership development and succession

Service Aspects

A service can be defined as the generation of an essentially intangible benefit, either on its own or as part of a tangible product, which satisfies an identified consumer need. Services have a number of particular characteristics, which need to be kept in mind both when trying to cover service related requirements in any RM approach, and when actually implementing a new RM approach such as the one proposed in this book within a given company. In the context of this book, the term 'services' is not used in the software engineering sense, but in a more general sense as opposed to 'products'.

Palmer identified the following pure service features [23]:

- intangibility (services cannot be touched);

- inseparability (production and consumption take place at the same time);

- variability (of both process and outcome);

- perishability (services cannot be stored for later consumption);

- no ownership (services cannot be possessed; no ownership is transferred due to their intangibility and perishability).

IMPLICATIONS FOR THE DEVELOPMENT OF SERVICE REQUIREMENTS

Although cost factors are far from being unimportant, there is overwhelming evidence that service quality is the single most important issue in running customer service operations successfully. It can be argued that service quality directly and indirectly affects profits in a significant way, as Zeithaml et al. [24] suggest.

They argue that high service quality leads to customer retention, which has shown to be cheaper in the long run than high levels of customer turnover. Also, long-term customers tend to buy larger volumes and higher price premium services and products. Very importantly, 'word-of-mouth' communications are affected in a positive way, being the most influential and convincing kind of communication in the field of services. If people talk positively about their experiences with the services delivered to other potential customers, market share is likely to grow, too. All this leads to higher possible margins [24].

By means of more 'offensive marketing', for example, putting aggressive promotional campaigns into practice, market share can be affected, a positive reputation enhanced and the service offer can be positioned in a way allowing for premium pricing strategies. All this can lead to higher sales levels. Both higher sales levels and higher achievable margins directly result in increased profits [24].

Hence service requirements have to be treated as an essential part of the portfolio of system requirements that will serve as the basis for the development of new systems.

Compared to the traditional marketing mix for products (4 Ps) – Product, Place (distribution), Promotion and Price – the marketing mix for services has to be expanded to account for additional complexity due to the specific features and characteristics of services. Zeithaml et al. argue that service customers, because services are intangible, will 'often be looking for any tangible cue to help them understand the nature of the service experience'. Therefore, they suggest that three additional elements – People, Physical evidence and Process – be included in marketing mix considerations [24].

Companies providing services, or systems including significant service components, need to carefully balance and optimize their specific services' marketing mix. All elements of the marketing mix must be consistent with the other elements and real life capacities or constraints.

For example, if a company promises (Promotion) high value, best-in-class service (Product) at the lowest price (Price) with incredible warranty conditions (Product), those communications are likely to result in customers' disbelief rather than higher usage rates of the service provided. Also, if a company advertises (Promotion) cheap (Price) and responsive service (Process) by well trained and friendly staff (People), but the service customers are actually experiencing not quite so cheap service with long queues, and they are served by unfriendly staff that do not seem to know what exactly they are doing, customers will be disappointed and lose confidence in all communications by this company. Both customer disbelief and disappointment will probably result in the customer searching the services needed elsewhere.

Especially in dealing with services, due to their intangibility, confidence-building appears to be very important. Therefore, the final marketing mix for market introduction must be agreed upon by all internal stakeholders to avoid harmful inconsistency between individual elements of the marketing mix, or between the marketing mix and real capacities and constraints of the company [25].

Services depend on a complex network of relationships between stakeholders including customers, providers, third parties, employees and technologies. From an SE viewpoint this denotes the imperative of using RM practices that can support enterprises to deliver the required services effectively (that is, meet or exceed stakeholder needs) and efficiently (that is, at an acceptable cost to both the stakeholders and the enterprise itself).

Zeithaml et al. proposed the 'gaps model of service quality' that can serve as a framework for considerations as to how superior service quality can be systematically created. This conceptual model is comprehensive and identifies sources of potential direct dissatisfaction, where customers do not get what they expect form a service (the 'Customer Gap' or 'Gap 5'); or sources of indirect dissatisfaction that lead to that perceived gap, where the enterprise does not deliver what the customer expects.

The process of closing the 'Customer Gap', that is, the difference between what the customer is expecting and what the customer perceives he gets from a service, can be subdivided into four internal company gaps or 'Provider Gaps' [24]:

- Provider Gap 1: not knowing what customers expect

- Provider Gap 2: not selecting the right service designs and standards

- Provider Gap 3: not delivering to service standards

- Provider Gap 4: not matching performance to promises

The 'Customer Gap' is the difference between the service a customer expects, for example, based on past experience, word-of-mouth communications, or promises made by the company in one form or another, and the delivered service, as perceived by the individual customer. Although it is argued to be resulting to a large extent from the four Provider Gaps and, therefore, is called 'Gap 5', the 'Customer Gap' is crucial to understanding better what this framework is all about, reducing this gap that is perceived by the customer and that will in one way or another influence his future behavior.

For example, a passenger using an airline will have built up in his mind (often subconsciously) a set of expectations from the service he will encounter along a number of criteria such as friendliness of staff, punctuality of the flight and cleanliness of the aircraft. These expectations may be mainly based on advertisements about the airline, word-of-mouth communications from other people who have already used the airline, and perhaps his own past experience with the airline or other airlines. During the actual delivery of the service, that is, the journey, the customer will experience or perceive the service to be as expected or possibly quite different than expected, that is, better or worse. The 'Customer Gap' means that perceived difference.

Based on the gap model of service quality, the 'Service Quality Cycle' was developed as a generic framework to proactively manage customer perceived service quality both effectively and efficiently. This framework needs to be adjusted to individual service operations depending on their specific context, and offers help in the development of service related requirements for a new system to be developed [25].

IMPLICATIONS FOR THE DEPLOYMENT OF A NEW RM PROCESS WITHIN A COMPANY

There are some lessons that can be learned for the implementation of change such as the deployment of the new RM approach proposed in this book. If you are an employee of your company and charged to deploy and run the RM process for a given program or project, some of the service aspects that were explained above will be helpful to enhance your efforts. In particular:

- Consider yourself as the RM service provider for your team.

- Keep all the participants in the RM process happy by doing your job well and treating them as your customers.

- Try to develop local experts or opinion leaders among these participants to promote a favorable attitude towards the RM process and your related efforts.

- By your good work and behavior, gain a positive reputation and create positive 'word-of-mouth' communications about your efforts, and the RM process in general.

- Make consistent and believable communications, and deliver as promised; for example when you ask a busy stakeholder for a time slot to elicit domain information with him, do respect the time slot that was agreed by arriving on time, being well prepared, and finishing the meeting as planned.

- Give your stakeholders every reason to build confidence in you and your work by delivering reliably and at good quality, as announced or agreed, never wasting their time.

The successful deployment of an RM approach including process, method and tool aspects on a larger scale such as for a transnational aircraft development program would require systematic service quality management [25].

If you are a service provider, who is contracted to deploy the RM process on behalf of a company that runs one or several programs or projects, you are in a very different situation. You are selling your service to deploy and run the RM process, and your direct customer is the company asking you to do the job. Therefore it is even more important for you to consider these service related aspects and provide excellent service quality in order to secure your business.

The Right Attitude – Dos and Don'ts

As already mentioned, human factors are certainly often underestimated and might quite possibly make the difference between a successful deployment of the RM process and sudden 'political martyrdom' during the attempt.

You will be a mature human being filled with the best intentions, and as such this section will not be of immediate concern to you. However, you may have to guide people that help you put in place the RM approach proposed in the next chapter.

Hence, the following recommendations might be of help for you as you make sure that everybody involved in the deployment of the RM process is behaving in the most constructive and helpful manner, in order to make the deployment efforts successful.

DOS (THIS LIST IS NOT EXHAUSTIVE)

- **Be upright and authentic**: People will notice if you are not, and they won't believe you in the future. Also, if you are authentic, you will feel better during your work, and hence work better.

- **Show honest respect**: Talk to and about everybody respectfully, whether they are around or not. People will notice, and there is nothing worse than to hear that someone you trust has talked badly about you behind your back. Make sure that you honestly respect people and do not just pretend.

- **Take people seriously**: The people you work with are all professionals and each of them knows things you don't, and can do things you can't. Don't just respect them as human beings, but also as professionals.

- **Be open-minded**: Sometimes the unexpected occurs and the person everybody thinks incapable of helping you, might just be the one who holds the information you need. You need to talk to people to find out: don't categorize them too quickly as unimportant or irrelevant for your work.

- **Create a climate of participation and ownership**: Make the participants in the RM process feel that they actually participate and help to make progress. Honor and praise their contributions, giving them a feeling of ownership of what was achieved, and how it was achieved.

- **Share praise collectively (if things go well)**: This will increase pride and ownership that the participants feel about the RM process and their contributions and, importantly, it will strongly motivate them to continue cooperating with you in the future.

- **Accept responsibility and shame personally (if things don't go well)**: You are driving the RM process; the other participants contribute to your efforts. It is a strong sign of good leadership if you are great enough to take the blame and don't pass it on to the people who were trying to help you achieve.

- **Invest in your employees/team members**: If you are leading a team, the team members are your most precious assets. Without them you can't do the job. Against them you definitely won't be able to do the job. With them you can achieve things you might not even imagine. Make sure they have the training they need, and importantly, they see that you also take their long-term career aspirations seriously, even if not directly related to your short-term RM work.

- **Empower your employees/team members**: If you send out your team members, give them the mandate and the support they need to do the work you expect them to do for you. Trust in them, and show them that you do. This will boost their motivation, as they will rightly feel valued and given responsibility.

- **Communicate well**: Use stakeholders' languages if possible. Find out how they prefer to communicate and when it is most convenient for them. Make sure you never waste their time. Communicate in a concise way. Make sure they have correctly understood you and vice versa.

- **Consider yourself a service provider**: Whether you are an internal employee or an external service provider for a program or project team, always try your best to deliver an excellent service in terms of RM. In larger scale programs or if you are indeed an external service provider, you absolutely should invest in the systematic management of your service quality.

DON'TS (THIS LIST IS NOT EXHAUSTIVE)

- **Don't be arrogant**: You are dependent on the people you work with. Arrogance never creates trustful, respectful and amicable relationships. If you are an arrogant type of person, start working on yourself immediately. Try to improve – or look for a job where you don't have to work with people.

- **Don't be pushy**: You should be careful never to push people around. It may work in the short run, but they will try to avoid you in the future.

- **Don't lie**: One of the most devastating things you can do to prevent trust relationships is to lie. Once people find out you lie, they will turn away from you, which will make your work impossible or at least very difficult.

- **Don't talk badly behind peoples' backs**: That is another 'reputation killer'. People are actually quite intelligent. When they see you 'slag off' other people behind their backs, they might wonder what you say about them behind theirs.

- **Don't claim successes personally**: Only bad leaders and poor managers claim that the team achievements occurred solely due to their own doing. This sends a strong message to all who participated that their contributions really were worthless, and that the only person properly contributing was you yourself.

- **Don't blame others in case of failures**: In some instances, this might even be worse than the above, especially if unjustified. Great leaders stand in front of their team and take the blame, if things did not work out as planned.

- **Don't speak RM jargon to people who are not familiar with it**: Have you ever spoken to a 'fanatical' stamp collector (no offense if you are one of them)? Now imagine you have barely heard of RM, and your team's Requirements Manager sits on your desk and speaks in RM abbreviations ... Since you need information from the participants in the RM process, you should try to speak their own language (both technical and native), if you can.

- **Don't assume because you have said something, everybody has understood you**: Have you ever had a misunderstanding in your own family, perhaps with your own spouse? Well presumably you have known each other for some time and you talk about things you both know. Now think about how easily misunderstandings do occur with people you don't know that well in the workplace. This is a difficult trap to avoid, but it pays to make an effort.

5

The RM Process

Chapter Summary

This chapter describes in detail a generic approach to RM that is both knowledge-driven and process-driven. It is intended for the development of complex or highly complex systems in a wide range of business contexts. This means that for simple systems, many of the proposed activities will be much less time-consuming and the needed tools to support the process and manage the created data may not have to be as sophisticated, since the data volumes for simple systems can be expected to be significantly lower.

Overview

The RM process as described in this chapter is a generic process that has to be instantiated – depending on the particular context and its complexity – at one or several layers of development, possibly within a complex extended enterprise. The process can be applied to a wide range of business and not-for-profit contexts alike. The purpose of the RM process is to establish all requirements of any relevant type for the particular context; and to keep them up-to-date over time.

The RM process consists of a number of workflows and their activities that are potentially concurrent and iterative. A process is an organized set of workflows and related activities which transform inputs into outputs. Process descriptions or models are essential to be able to reuse and continuously improve knowledge in general, and this applies also to the RM process itself.

A workflow consists of a number of related activities, which are integrated components of one or several workflows. Both workflows and their related activities can be conducted concurrently with a number of different stakeholders.

This reflects reality insofar as the RM process is not usually a strictly sequential, one-off process with all needed participants just waiting for the requirements manager to turn up. In real life, people are not always available and many iterations and concurrent loops may be necessary throughout the relevant parts of the extended enterprise.

Also, the RM process does not suddenly stop at an early stage of the system development, but it continues, although usually at a much lower level, throughout the entire life cycle of a program or system. This is important because whenever a change of an existing system is needed, we have to be able to analyze the impacts of the change and systematically control the preparation and implementation of this change.

The output of the generic RM process is a new or updated set of validated requirements. The subject of these requirements, as well as their level of granularity and detail, will depend on the purpose and organization of the team or the individual for which the generic RM process is instantiated. The resulting requirements will specify aspects of a program, project or system in a given context.

Figure 5.1 provides a high-level overview of the generic RM process. The light bulb represents some new idea or significant change in a particular context, which leads you to develop new requirements – for instance, the intended launch of a new aircraft development program, or the extension of a secondary school building complex.

The two main parts of the RM process are the Requirements Development (RD) process and the Requirements Change Management (RCM) process. RD is the process of developing requirements. It can be subdivided into a number of potentially concurrent and iterative phases: Elicitation, Analysis and Negotiation, Documentation and Validation. The output of this process is a new set of validated requirements.

RCM is the process of managing changes to requirements over the entire life cycle of the program or system. The principal RCM activities are change control and change impact assessment. RCM requires traceability information to be recorded, that is, specific links among requirements, the sources of requirements, the system design, and planned actions and evidence of validation and verification activities. The output of this process is an updated set of validated requirements.

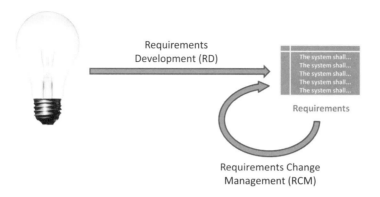

Requirements
Development (RD)

The system shall...
The system shall...
The system shall...
The system shall...
The system shall...

Requirements

Requirements Change
Management (RCM)

Figure 5.1   High-level overview of the generic RM process

Figure 5.2 provides a more detailed view of the generic RM process, showing the four steps of the RM process. This is not to say that these steps take place one after the other, strictly sequentially, and only once. Rather, as was mentioned above, the generic RM process usually takes place in an iterative and concurrent manner due to certain circumstances in a given context.

These circumstances may be that the involved relevant stakeholders and domain experts are not available as and when needed following the RM process. Also, required information such as higher level input requirements or the outcomes of a simulation or technology research study may not be available when needed, while following the process. As a result, specific parts of the RM process may have to be conducted with different participants at different moments in time, or they will have to be revisited or repeated, once the required information becomes available.

At the same time, there may not be time to wait at each stage until you can complete every workflow exhaustively. Rather, the person conducting the RM process may be forced to continue the process as far as possible, knowingly and intentionally allowing certain gaps in the needed information, until this information becomes available. However, care must be taken not to risk significant corrective rework.

For example, if a relevant stakeholder is not available for three weeks, you could already elicit and capture the needed information from all other identified relevant stakeholders and domain experts, and then go through the same workflows and activities with him when he is available again.

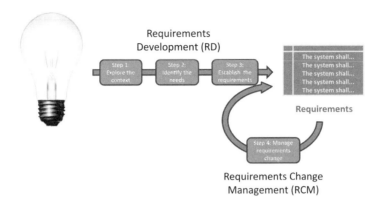

Figure 5.2   The four steps of the generic RM process

The RM process has to allow for the above circumstances, and needs to be sufficiently flexible and reliable to cope with them because this reflects reality.

In the following, all four steps will be explained in detail, discussing each of the corresponding workflows. For each workflow, all needed activities as well as their inputs and outputs will be described, stating the involvement of participants where applicable. Also, references will be made to suitable techniques and tools that can support these workflows and activities as appropriate. These techniques and tools are described in more detail in Chapter 6, and a mapping from the RM process workflows that will be described in this chapter to the recommended techniques and tools that can best support them is provided in Appendix G.

Requirements Development

The RD process is subdivided into three steps: 'Step 1 – Explore the context', 'Step 2 – Identify the needs', and 'Step 3 – Establish the requirements'. Although these three steps are potentially iterative and concurrent, they can only be finalized or closed one after the other in their sequential order. For example, you cannot consider that you have a complete set of requirements before you have finished elaborating all underlying needs.

As you go through the steps of the RD process, it is of utmost importance to record relevant traceability information and to keep this information under an appropriate form of configuration management.

For example, if you develop a requirement based on a higher level of input requirements, you should immediately establish the link between both requirements, or if you are not working in a requirements database yet you should at least record the source reference. It only takes a moment to establish this traceability while you still work on the requirement, because then you exactly know where the source or related information is located. It takes much longer and is prone to errors if someone else or even you have to establish this traceability later.

It is almost certain that you will need the relevant traceability information later on, because it tremendously facilitates the analysis and validation activities, and it is also the necessary basis for the RCM process once the requirements have been established for the first time. This is so because the recorded traceability information enables change impact analyses.

Furthermore, you should aim to complete each step with the appropriate involvement of all identified relevant stakeholders and domain experts before you start the next step in order to keep corrective rework to a minimum. On the other hand, if a particular relevant stakeholder is on a holiday for two weeks, you should not stop all activities until he returns. The RM process described in this section explicitly allows for the flexibility that is required in such cases.

A summary checklist of the entire RD process is provided in Appendix B.

STEP 1 – EXPLORE THE CONTEXT

The first step consists of the following three workflows: (1) 'Identify and review relevant documentation', (2) 'Identify and map stakeholders' and (3) 'Elicit and capture relevant context information'. The latter workflow needs direct involvement of relevant stakeholders and domain experts, as marked in Figure 5.3 (a symbol of a person is used and the workflow is written in bold font).

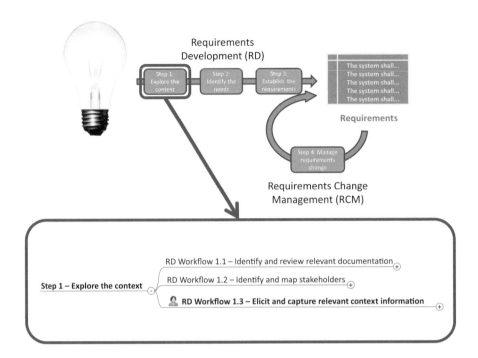

Figure 5.3   Explore the context

RD workflow 1.1 – identify and review relevant documentation

The first workflow is about finding out what existing documentation and similar sources are relevant for the current context and available and reviewing them in order to have a good overview and understanding of this specific context – even before talking in detail to any stakeholders.

This is important since you need stakeholder involvement in the RM process, and you do not want to put them off by wasting their time. Asking them obvious questions that you could have easily answered yourself by reading the corresponding procedural document, which may be available on the company's intranet, may seriously annoy them. You should make sure that you use their precious time as effectively as possible, adding the greatest value to the RM process.

Table 5.1 displays the activities of this workflow, as well as their inputs and outputs. There is no intended participant involvement, other than asking the people around you for the right places to find the documentation you are looking for. Hence, no participants are marked in the table.

Table 5.1   Identify and review relevant documentation

Activity	Input	Output
Identify and review relevant procedural documents	Relevant procedural documents	Relevant procedural documents identified and reviewed
Identify and review relevant regulation and legislation	Relevant regulation and legislation	Relevant regulation and legislation identified and reviewed
Identify and review relevant studies and publications	Relevant studies and publications	Relevant studies and publications identified and reviewed
Identify and review relevant lessons learned and good practice	Relevant lessons learned and good practice	Relevant lessons learned and good practice identified and reviewed
Identify and review requirements from relevant previous projects or programs	Relevant previous requirements	Reusable requirements identified and reviewed
Identify and review existing input requirements from potential stakeholders	Existing input requirements	Input requirements identified and reviewed
Record relevant key information and sources	Relevant documentation identified and reviewed	Relevant key information and sources recorded

The relevant documentation you need to identify and review, if available, is likely to consist of procedural documents, specific regulation and legislation, standards, studies and publications, lessons learned and identified good practice, requirements from previous projects or programs, as well as your input requirements that may have already been established by your current stakeholders.

All such relevant documentation should be referenced by you, and the main information you deem relevant should be summarized, or in some cases the document stored for later use. For example, you could save a previous requirements document from a similar project in a dedicated working folder for your current project.

Remember that the aim here is not to spend a lot of time going through all possible types of documents that may have something to do with your current project in detail. Rather you should try to see this workflow as an opportunity to save time for you and the participants in the RM process, by not 're-inventing the wheel', where there is already something useful documented.

Maybe there are some informal customer expectations available from customer focus groups or in service support reports; or you are participating in a bidding process based on a set of input requirements. Any such information is of course very useful to review before we actually take our stakeholders' time.

Just a few words on input requirements that your stakeholders may already have established for you, when you start developing your own requirements at your level. In principle, input requirements can come via two routes: (1) relevant stakeholders can propose the allocation of specific requirements to you ('push' principle) and (2) you can contact identified relevant stakeholders and proactively 'trawl' for requirements ('pull' principle).

In the first case, you should review the requirements proposed for allocation and either agree with the proposed allocation, or where necessary negotiate with the relevant stakeholder to reach an agreement. This may be necessary if you do not understand a requirement, if you think it is not relevant for you, that is, if you suspect a wrong allocation, or if a requirement is not of good quality and needs reformulating. Early negotiation of input requirements leads to a better understanding of these, and an early identification of mis-allocations, problems and risks, as well as constraints from other teams.

In the second case, you may have to proactively contact specific relevant stakeholders and ask them for your input requirements – or even elicit the input requirements with them, if they have not been able to formulate and allocate any input requirements to you yet, for whatever reason. In this case, just follow the relevant parts of this RM process. And remember that it is in your best interests to have good input requirements, even if it may not be your direct responsibility to produce them. It is time well spent and your help will certainly be appreciated by your stakeholder.

When reusing existing requirements from previous projects or programs, you should take care to analyze every single requirement (to be reused) for relevance, necessity, need for adaptation to the new context, and its source. Also, you need to decide how the reused requirement can be updated if the original requirement (in a different context) is changed, or if this does not matter.

This workflow can be effectively enhanced by brainstorming and mind mapping techniques, which can be supported by mind mapping and spreadsheet tools.

RD workflow 1.2 – identify and map stakeholders

This workflow is about finding out and recording with whom we need to talk so as to be able to develop our requirements. Stakeholders are individuals, groups or organizations who will be affected in some way by the development, sale, delivery, support, operational use or disposal of a system to be developed, and therefore have a direct or indirect influence on the system requirements.

They include end-users of the system, clients who are paying for the system, managers and others involved in the organizational processes influenced by the system, engineers responsible for the system development and maintenance, customers of the organization who will use the system to provide some services, external bodies such as regulators or certification authorities, and so on.

Those stakeholders out of the many possible stakeholders that have been declared to be the official stakeholders within a given project or program are the relevant stakeholders. They usually have to validate the requirements and sign them off.

Domain experts, on the other hand, may be stakeholders, or unconcerned who might not even be part of the project or program in question, but who have some relevant expertise or experience in the field at hand. They are often overlooked and not considered in order to save time, or because they are simply forgotten. Yet, in many cases, they actually have significant inputs to contribute. Table 5.2 displays the activities of this workflow, indicating their inputs and outputs.

Table 5.2   Identify and map stakeholders

Activity	Input	Output
Identify relevant stakeholders	Relevant key information Recommendations	Relevant stakeholders identified
Identify relevant domain experts	Relevant key information Recommendations	Relevant domain experts identified
Map the relevant stakeholders and domain experts	Relevant stakeholders and domain experts identified	Relevant stakeholders and domain experts mapped

Based on the previously recorded, relevant key information, and perhaps recommendations by people you talk to, this workflow can be undertaken in isolation, without any formal participants.

This said, in practice the stakeholder map is usually initiated alone, but then, during discussions with some of the identified stakeholders, you will often identify additional stakeholders that you may wish to add to your stakeholder map. This tends to be the case especially for domain experts, since they will not necessarily be stated in any relevant program documentation because they may not be part of the program in question.

The resulting stakeholder map may have to be updated later on in the process when you come across any additional recommendations of relevant stakeholders or domain experts by the people you are meeting, and occasionally when identified stakeholders leave their position and are replaced.

As with the previous workflow, this workflow can be effectively enhanced by brainstorming and mind mapping techniques, which are supported by mind mapping and spreadsheet tools.

RD workflow 1.3 – elicit and capture relevant context information

This workflow is about meeting relevant people, who either will have to validate or sign off your requirements later on (relevant stakeholders), or can contribute to your work of eliciting and capturing relevant domain knowledge or information (domain experts).

This workflow is very important because it helps you achieve the necessary foundation for a complete and consistent set of requirements in the end, and also to obtain the buy-in of the people who have to sign off your requirements later on by having them participate in the process of developing the requirements and offering them intermediate opportunities to have an influence on this process. Table 5.3 displays the activities of this workflow, indicating the involvement of the participants, as well as inputs and outputs of all activities.

Table 5.3   Elicit and capture relevant context information

Activity	Input	Output
Prepare sessions with relevant stakeholders and domain experts	Relevant stakeholders and domain experts mapped	Relevant stakeholders and domain experts invited to sessions
Initiate the capture of context information based on the recorded relevant key information	Relevant key information and sources recorded	Initial context information captured
Extend the captured context information with the relevant stakeholders and domain experts	Initial context information captured	Context information completed
Document how the context information was extended by who until completion	Initial context information captured	Context information traceable to its sources

Short meetings of one to two hours should be scheduled with all identified relevant stakeholders and domain experts individually. Try to schedule these meetings in the light of the participants' availability and convenience, taking into consideration any local customs and preferences.

Some may wish to have their meeting jointly with other stakeholders you wish to invite, or in fact people you had not previously identified. If specifically requested, this is fine and should be accommodated for, but in general it is very helpful to have individual meetings so that undivided attention can be given to each participant.

These meetings must be well prepared beforehand by using and visualizing the context information that could be obtained previously, for example, from the existing context documentation.

During the meetings, this initially prepared and any subsequently captured context information can be shown to other participants, who can then comment and confirm it or contradict it, and help you improve the structure of the information. You should keep a record of who contributed which part of the information, and who disagreed with what others had said, and for what reasons.

As you go about eliciting the domain knowledge on which you will base your requirements later in the process, you should make use of any relevant or helpful types of modeling, simulation, and analyses. Also, it is often at this stage that you may become aware of additional people you might want to speak to. This may be the case when already identified stakeholders recommend during your discussions with them that you should ask specific other domain experts regarding certain relevant aspects.

This workflow can be effectively enhanced by techniques such as brainstorming, mind mapping, diagramming user interactions, functional analysis, safety analysis, why-why-analysis, scenario analysis, use case analysis, and walkthrough. It is recommended that these techniques be supported by mind mapping, spreadsheet and modeling tools.

STEP 2 – IDENTIFY THE NEEDS

The second step consists of the following three workflows: (1) 'Derive needs', (2) 'Analyze and update needs' and (3) 'Validate needs'. The last workflow requires direct involvement of relevant stakeholders and domain experts, as marked in Figure 5.4.

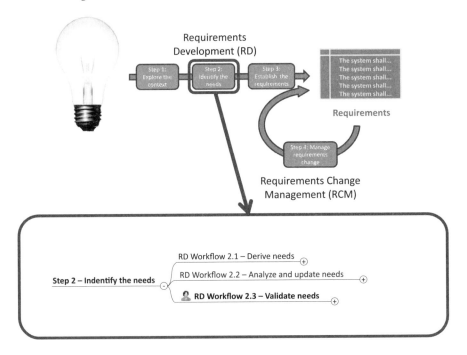

Figure 5.4   Identify the needs

All workflows of Step 2 can be greatly enhanced by using mind mapping techniques and a dedicated mind mapping tool.

RD workflow 2.1 – derive needs

This workflow is about translating all the information and knowledge you have captured regarding your problem context into one coherent set of high-level needs. If you have explored the problem context using a mind map, you will have captured and structured different sorts of concerns, business process aspects, actors, scenarios, functions, use cases, and other relevant models that have some impact on your problem space. This structured yet 'messy' information is of different levels of granularity and detail. Therefore it has to be used to formulate a list of high-level needs that summarize the entire 'problem space', for which you ultimately want to find one or several alternative solutions that satisfy your needs.

This workflow is important because it makes explicit the underlying external and internal needs that are to be satisfied. Table 5.4 displays the activities of this workflow, including their inputs and outputs.

Table 5.4   Derive needs

Activity	Input	Output
Establish a set of needs	Context information completed and traceable to its sources	Set of needs established
Establish traceability from each need to the underlying context information	Set of needs established	Set of needs traceable to the underlying context information

Establishing traceability from the needs into the domain knowledge from which you have derived them is essential, because this greatly facilitates the analysis and validation of your needs in the short term, and enables the continued use and efficient reuse of the domain knowledge in the longer term.

Each such need has one or several relevant stakeholders and possibly domain experts associated with it, namely the ones who originally gave you the captured problem space information, based on which you have derived the need.

Needs can address one or several constraints on a new system to be developed, or the project or program that is conducted to develop the new system, or any capabilities or characteristics of the new system in general. However, needs are not detailed requirements yet but rather high-level statements. This means that they are likely to be very vague, not easily measurable, and they are usually open regarding any possible solutions.

Needs can be considered to be the formalized summary of the 'problem space' before entering into the 'solution space' by developing the goals and later requirements. This solution space (defined by the goals and requirements) specifies the 'allowable space' in which alternative solutions can be identified that will satisfy the derived needs.

It is good practice to go through the entire context information that was previously captured, create one need per major topic, and link from that need to the parts of the context knowledge from which the need was derived. You have completed the workflow when (1) you have covered the entire context knowledge that was captured, (2) you are happy with the formulation of each individual need and (3) each need is linked to where it originated from in the problem space.

Therefore it can be said that one key aspect of this workflow is the establishment of traceability within the problem space that can later be used for analysis and validation purposes at the need, goal and requirement levels.

RD workflow 2.2 – analyze and update needs

This workflow is about making sure that the established list of high-level needs are of good quality in terms of their correctness, completeness and consistency. All should be traceable, there should be no overlapping or partly duplicated needs, and any conflicts have to be identified and resolved.

This is very important because the list of needs will be the basis for the development of goal hierarchies and later requirements that will specify the solution space. Also, both the analysis and any necessary corrections of the derived needs will take considerably less effort and time, and therefore cost less if it is done at this early stage, as opposed to identifying problems later when the goals or even requirements have already been formulated. Table 5.5 displays the activities of this workflow, including their inputs and outputs.

Table 5.5   Analyze and update needs

Activity	Input	Output
Analyze each need individually	Set of needs established Traceability of needs established	Quality gaps of individual needs identified
Update each need as needed	Quality gaps of individual needs identified	Needs updated individually
Analyze the complete set of needs	Needs updated individually	Conflicts and duplications identified
Update the complete set of needs as needed	Conflicts and duplications identified	Conflicts of needs documented Duplications of needs removed

First, each of the needs has to be reviewed individually, whether it is well expressed, that is, clear and understandable, and linked to its origin in the captured context knowledge. Then, the entire set of needs has to be reviewed in its entirety to ensure that the list is complete, of a comparable level of granularity and detail, and free of conflicts. Any identified conflicts will be recorded and duplications removed from the set of needs.

RD workflow 2.3 – validate needs

This workflow is about having your relevant stakeholders validate the first intermediate outcome of your requirements development efforts. By validating the list of needs, they will give their agreement that you have established a complete and consistent high-level summary of the problems to be solved.

This is important because it gives you the confidence that you are on the right track, even if there may be some corrections to do at this stage. Also, the workflow contributes to the buy-in of the relevant stakeholders, because they are given the opportunity to validate this intermediate outcome of your requirements work. Table 5.6 displays the activities of this workflow including their inputs and outputs, as well as the involvement of other participants.

Table 5.6   Validate needs

Activity	Input	Output
Prepare the validation of the needs	Complete set of analyzed and updated needs	Relevant stakeholders and domain experts invited to sessions
Drive the validation by the relevant stakeholders and domain experts	Relevant stakeholders and domain experts invited to sessions	Validation of needs completed
Record the outcome of the validation	Validation of needs completed	Outcome of needs validation recorded
Implement any necessary changes	Changes necessary as agreed during the validation of needs	Necessary changes implemented
Record the implementation of any necessary changes	Necessary changes implemented	Implemented changes recorded

Once the list of needs has been analyzed and updated as necessary, the relevant stakeholders are invited to individual sessions where you should talk them through their needs in detail in order to get their feedback. They should also be given the opportunity to look at the other needs of which they are not themselves the relevant stakeholders. This will help increase the confidence that the set of needs is in fact consistent.

Alternatively, this validation can also be driven via video or telephone conference, or even via email. For globally dispersed teams, this may be the most economical way in the light of limited travel budgets. However, you have to be confident that the relevant stakeholders fully understand what you have done and agree with your outcomes, before they validate the needs you have derived.

STEP 3 – ESTABLISH THE REQUIREMENTS

The third step consists of the following six workflows: (1) 'Create goal hierarchies', (2) 'Analyze and update goal hierarchies', (3) 'Validate goal hierarchies', (4) 'Write requirements', (5) 'Analyze and update requirements' and (6) 'Validate requirements'. The third and sixth workflows need direct involvement of relevant stakeholders and domain experts, as marked in Figure 5.5.

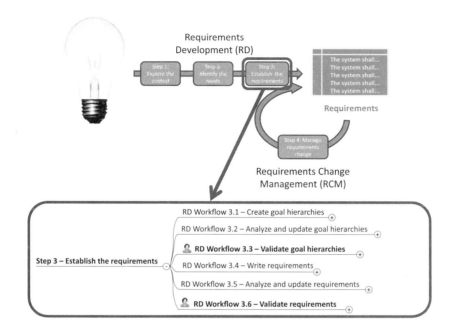

Figure 5.5   Establish the requirements

RD workflow 3.1 – create goal hierarchies

The first workflow of Step 3 is about determining for each validated need how this need can be best satisfied. By building goal hierarchies you can sometimes prepare quite complex graphs of goals and sub-goals that are of increasing level of detail, until you arrive at root goals. The latter are quite detailed goals that you think should not be further broken down into sub-goals. The assumption is that if all root goals of one need are met, then this need can be considered as satisfied.

This workflow is important because it leads from the list of identified high-level needs to a much more detailed level of concrete root goals that can subsequently be used as the basis to write corresponding requirements. Table 5.7 displays the activities of this workflow, as well as their inputs and outputs.

Table 5.7   Create goal hierarchies

Activity	Input	Output
Create a goal hierarchy for each validated need	A set of validated needs	One goal hierarchy per validated need
Identify all root goals in all goal hierarchies	One goal hierarchy per validated need	All root goals identified

The creation of goal hierarchies before even starting to write requirements is quite an important concept, because it takes much less time to create, analyze and update goals that are not very formal in nature, as opposed to much more detailed requirements.

Furthermore, it is easier at this stage to identify and resolve conflicts, remove duplications and increase consistency. Figure 5.6 shows a generic goal hierarchy that was created for an identified need.

For example, if one of the validated needs was the following:

The Aircraft needs to be perceived as setting a new standard in passenger comfort during all operational flight phases.

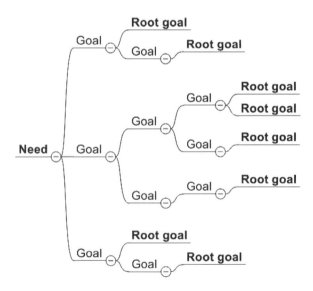

Figure 5.6   A generic goal hierarchy

Then, some of the first level goals in the associated goal hierarchy for this need could be:

- *'Reduce cabin noise levels.'*

- *'Reduce fuel particles in the cabin air.'*

- *'Increase legroom.'*

- *'Make available flexible lighting.'*

- *'Use surface materials that promote feelings of well-being when touched.'*

- *'Provide sufficient seat width for obese passengers.'*

- *'Provide sufficient length of seat belt for obese passengers.'*

- *'Enable complete retraction of arm rests into the seat.'*

These goals would have to be further broken down, if needed with the help of domain experts and using modeling where helpful, until you arrive at a very detailed and quantifiable level that can then be used as the basis for writing your requirements later on in the RM process.

For instance, regarding the first goal 'Reduce cabin noise levels' it would have to be explored and decided what noise levels are actually perceived to be acceptable per operational phase, and in the light of competitors' products, so that the goal contributes to the achievement of the underlying need.

Even in cases where it seems hard to quantify, there is always a way around it. For instance, focus group meetings or questionnaires can be used with sample groups of passengers in order to measure certain perceptions. Also, a number of other analyses can be used very effectively to identify during which operational phases, in which use cases or scenarios certain goals are valid, as opposed to being valid all the time. Often, domain experts would make a decision based on their own professional judgement, and this may be as good a concrete and measurable value as you will get.

The completeness and consistency of goals and (later in the process) requirements is practically impossible to achieve for complex systems. The important thing is to get to a sufficient level of completeness and consistency, based on multiple analyses from many viewpoints and in the light of the experience of all participants in the process.

This workflow can be effectively enhanced by mind mapping techniques, plus diagramming user interactions, functional analysis, safety analyses, why-why analysis, scenario analysis, use case analysis and walkthrough techniques. Also traceability has to be established between the goal hierarchies that were created and their multiple sources such as models or studies. These techniques are best supported by dedicated mind mapping, modeling and spreadsheet tools.

RD workflow 3.2 – analyze and update goal hierarchies

This workflow is about making sure that the established goal hierarchies are of good quality in terms of their correctness, completeness and consistency. Any duplications of goals have to be eliminated, and conflicts identified and resolved.

This is very important because the requirements will be based on the identified root goals within each goal hierarchy. Also, both analysis and any necessary corrections of the established goals will take considerably less effort and time and therefore cost less at this stage, as opposed to identifying problems later, when the requirements have already been formulated. Table 5.8 displays the activities of this workflow, as well as their inputs and outputs.

Table 5.8   Analyze and update goal hierarchies

Activity	Input	Output
Analyze each goal individually	Complete list of individual goals	Each goal analyzed individually
Update each goal as needed	Each goal analyzed individually	Each individual goal updated as needed
Analyze each goal hierarchy individually	All established goal hierarchies	Each goal hierarchy analyzed individually
Update each goal hierarchy as needed	Each goal hierarchy analyzed individually	Each goal hierarchy updated as needed
Analyze the complete set of goal hierarchies	Complete set of goal hierarchies	Complete set of goal hierarchies analyzed
Update the complete set of goal hierarchies as needed	Complete set of goal hierarchies analyzed	Complete set of analyzed and updated goal hierarchies

Each of the goals and sub-goals in all goal hierarchies for all validated needs has to be analyzed or reviewed individually to see whether it is well expressed, that is, clear and understandable. Then all goal hierarchies have to be analyzed or reviewed one by one, to check that they are correct, complete and consistent. In particular, the question has to be asked whether all identified root goals together, if achieved, actually satisfy the underlying need. Finally, it has to be made sure that all needs have been covered in that way, and that duplications and conflicts between goals from different goal hierarchies have been identified and addressed.

This workflow can be effectively enhanced by mind mapping techniques that are supported by mind mapping and spreadsheet tools.

RD workflow 3.3 – validate goal hierarchies

This workflow is about having your relevant stakeholders validate the second key intermediate outcome of your requirements development efforts. By validating the goal hierarchies for the identified needs that they have already validated, they will give their agreement to the way you propose that each need could be satisfied, and the green light that the requirements can now be formulated based on the identified root goals. Table 5.9 displays the activities of this workflow, including their inputs and outputs, as well as the involvement of participants.

Table 5.9   Validate goal hierarchies

Activity	Input	Output
Prepare the validation of the goal hierarchies	Complete set of analyzed and updated goal hierarchies	Relevant stakeholders and domain experts invited to sessions
Drive the validation by the relevant stakeholders and domain experts	Relevant stakeholders and domain experts invited to sessions	Validation of goal hierarchies completed
Record the outcome of the validation	Validation of goal hierarchies completed	Outcome of the validation of goal hierarchies recorded
Implement any necessary changes	Changes necessary as agreed during the validation of goal hierarchies	Necessary changes implemented
Record the implementation of any necessary changes	Necessary changes implemented	Implemented changes recorded

This is important because it gives you the confidence that you are on the right track, even if there may be some corrections to do at this stage. In addition to that, this workflow strongly contributes to the buy-in of the relevant stakeholders, because they are given the opportunity to validate the outcome of your requirements work at another key stage on the way towards completing the requirements. This will also greatly facilitate the validation of the requirements later on.

Once all goal hierarchies have been analyzed and updated as needed, the relevant stakeholders are invited to individual sessions, where you should talk them through the developed goal hierarchies in detail in order to get their feedback. They should also be given the opportunity to look at the other goal hierarchies of which they are not themselves the relevant stakeholders. This will help increase the confidence that the set of goal hierarchies is in fact consistent, or at least identify any issues that had been overlooked despite the previous analyses or reviews.

Alternatively, this validation can also be driven via video or telephone conference, or even via email; as for global teams, this may be the most economical way in the light of limited travel budgets. However, as mentioned before, you have to be confident that the relevant stakeholders fully understand what you have done and agree with your outcomes, before they validate the goals that you have developed with their help.

Just as the previous workflow, this workflow can be effectively enhanced by mind mapping techniques that are supported by mind mapping and spreadsheet tools.

RD workflow 3.4 – write requirements

This workflow is about actually writing your requirements and completing any additional information in the form of attributes and links; based on the work previously performed, or in direct response to input requirements that are allocated to you directly by a stakeholder or customer. Also, in some cases you may be able to reuse existing requirements from similar contexts, in which case you still need to make sure that these requirements are well written and contain all the information you need for your specific context.

This is important because the resulting set of requirements, be they newly written or reused, will become the basis for your work, or for your contract with a supplier or customer. Whatever it is that will be developed based on these requirements will be wrong if the requirements are wrong. Therefore this workflow is crucial. Table 5.10 displays the activities of this workflow, including their inputs and outputs.

In larger organizations and/or for highly complex systems, requirements would usually be managed in a dedicated requirements database that is supported by a suitable software tool and reflects a common data-model. Such a requirements database enables the participants in the RM process to manage all requirements individually as objects, including any related information in terms of attributes and possibly links to related objects that are also stored within the requirements database.

The following criteria will both help writing good requirements in the first place, and facilitate the analysis of requirements prior to their validation. The criteria are divided into two levels, that is, the individual requirements level and the set of requirements level.

The former level is about producing high-quality individual requirements, whereas the latter level is about complete and consistent sets of requirements, for example, in the form of high-quality requirements documents. The criteria for both levels are summarized in Appendices E and F respectively.

Table 5.10   Write requirements

Activity	Input	Output
For each validated root goal write one new requirement or reuse a suitable existing requirement	Validated root goals Identified reusable requirements	Own requirements captured based on validated root goals
For each identified input requirement write one new requirement or reuse a suitable existing requirement	Identified input requirements Identified reusable requirements	Own requirements captured based on input requirements
Establish traceability from each new requirement and reused requirement to the respective source	Own requirements captured	Own requirements linked to sources
Complete all mandatory attribute information for each new and reused requirement	Own requirements linked to sources	Own requirements completed

Check that each individual requirement is:

- necessary

- attainable

- clear and unambiguous

- verifiable

- not premature design

- complete

Each requirement has to be necessary, that is, there has to be an identified stakeholder with an underlying, justified need. A requirement will have a certain priority, which can change over time. But even low priority requirements have to be necessary in the sense that they have to be stated. Think about what would be the worst that could happen if you left the requirement out.

Each requirement has to be realistic and achievable in terms of the laws of physics and domain experience. Technical feasibility as well as budget and schedule constraints should be considered, but they should not prevent you from stating challenging requirements. Often, in the beginning of a new development program for a highly complex system, the needed technologies to satisfy some of the requirements will not be available yet. If something is required it has to be stated as a requirement, even if we cannot satisfy it yet. At least this helps to make that very fact explicit.

Requirements, in particular the requirement statements, have to be clear and unambiguous in order to avoid misunderstandings. They shall be kept as simple as possible, show relevant punctuation, consist of only one sentence per requirement statement (and only one requirement per sentence), avoid noun clusters and use tabular layout where appropriate.

For each requirement you should think about how the design, and later the product should be verified, so that you can decide whether you consider that the requirement has been satisfied. Therefore each requirement has to be formulated in a way that it is verifiable; and you should have proposed means of design and product verification in the corresponding attributes of the requirement.

The requirement should never constrain the solution space more than necessary at its level. Solutions should only be imposed by means of requirements if this is really a necessary constraint, for example if a stakeholder explicitly needs a detailed specific solution.

Each requirement has to contain all needed statement components, mandatory attribute information and links or references in line with the established requirements data-model. You may wish to write individual requirement statements split into their components following the structure shown in Table 5.11, and fill in every component that is relevant for a given requirement.

Table 5.11   Parsing requirement statements into components (adapted from Halligan, 2010) [26]

Component	Example
Actor	Any single fuel pump
Condition(s) for action	on ground
Action	shall be replaceable
Constraint(s) of action	by one 'level 2' maintainer
Object of action	-
Refinement / source of object	without having to drain the tank
Refinement / destination of action	within 20 minutes
Other	-

Table 5.12 shows a number of example requirement statements from the aerospace context related to an aircraft, a program, a training module, an aircraft subsystem, and an aircraft structure component.

Table 5.12   Example requirement statements

The **MZV aircraft**, with the Extended Range option package, shall be able to carry XX passengers over a distance of YYYYY km.
The **MZV program** shall define NRC and RC targets for all MZV aircraft variants and standard option packages by Maturity Gate XY.
The **MZV training** for flight crews of the MZV aircraft (all variants and standard option packages) shall take the following number of days: • 5 days if not qualified for MZV company aircraft, • 2 days if qualified for MZV aircraft family, • 1 day if qualified for MZV aircraft.
The **Air Conditioning System** shall regulate hot air temperature discharge by a closed control loop based on bypass air modulation.
The **Air Conditioning System** shall achieve the mix of hot and cold air by means of a valve.
The **Air Conditioning System** shall make sure that the valve is in the full closed position in case of failure.
The **Load Management System** shall compute the optimum load positioning taking into account the following criteria: • Characteristics of load items, • Air delivery sequence, • Any load restrictions, when operated from the manual work station.
The **Vertical Tail Plane**, during landing and take-off on a 90-ft wide runway, shall sustain a crosswind component of: • 35 kts for a braking coefficient > 0.4 • 15 kts for a braking coefficient $0.25 < x < 0.4$

As a general rule, no requirement should be repeated if it has already been expressed somewhere else in the requirements database, in order to avoid unnecessary costs without adding value. You should refer to the source of such a requirement (using a 'source' attribute) if the requirement in question is not in a requirements database, or directly link to it if it is. Only in some special cases it may be necessary to repeat a requirement, for example, where complete sets of requirements have to be passed to suppliers (in the form of a document) that do not have access to the original requirement in question. However, never should a requirement be repeated in the same requirements document.

If identical requirements are used in a number of requirements databases and linking among them is not enabled, these requirements can be mirrored, that is, copied into other databases to allow for local traceability within these other requirements databases. This is often the case when requirements are developed outside the requirements database using specific methodologies, and subsequently managed within the database, or within the extended enterprise between a customer company and a supplier company.

For example, the customer company may manage a requirements document in their requirements database for a given project, and these requirements will be copied into the supplier's requirements database; so that they can link from their own more detailed requirements and other related information to the copy of the customer requirements.

Table 5.13 provides a selection of useful requirement attributes. In order to ensure consistency and reusability of requirements and their associated information, a common data model would normally be implemented in the requirements database.

For instance, some attributes may offer a selection of pre-defined values to pick from: for example, the requirement status may offer the values of 'proposed', 'analyzed' and 'deleted'. This is necessary in order to analyze the status of the requirements work within the entire requirements database.

Table 5.13   A selection of useful requirement attributes

Attribute	Comment
Unique ID	Each requirement must have a unique identifier.
Created by	The author of the requirement.
Object type	In some requirements database systems the distinction is made between requirements and other objects that are managed.
Requirement statement	The requirement statement is the core of the textual requirement. It formulates what is actually required.
Rationale	The reason or justification for a requirement. Often this information contains the experience and know-how of the author of the requirement.
Owner	The owner of a requirement is not the stakeholder of the requirement, but the person in charge of its development and management. For example, the owner would drive the validation of his requirement by the designated relevant stakeholder.
Stakeholder	The relevant stakeholder(s) should be stated in this attribute, that is, the designated stakeholder(s).
Requirement type	This attribute would let you select from a set of established categories of requirements, for example, 'functional' versus 'non-functional' requirements with a number of subcategories; or 'product' versus 'enabling product' versus 'process' requirements.
Scenario	Reference number of the scenario during which the requirement is necessary.
Use case	Reference number of the use cases during which the requirement is necessary.

Table 5.13   *Concluded*

Attribute	Comment
Function	Reference number of applicable functions from the identified functional tree (functional requirements only).
Fit criterion	Criterion that needs to be given in order to consider the requirement as being satisfied by the design and/or the system to be developed.
Version	This attribute contains version information such as which requirement component was changed, when, and due to what decision.
Priority	For example: 'key', 'secondary', and 'unimportant'; 'order winners', 'qualifiers', and 'less important'; or 'essential', 'important', and 'nice to have'.
Additional information	Here, any additional information of relevance can be stored and managed. This should facilitate the understanding of the requirement by any reader.
Assumption	Any major assumptions on which the requirement is based should be stated here. By linking this kind of information to project or program risks, risk management can be greatly enhanced. If such an assumption does not hold true, all concerned requirements can be immediately identified via the established traceability, and analyzed for any impacts.
Source	If a requirement is directly based on a source document that cannot be linked to from the requirements database, the source reference should be given in this attribute.
Requirement status	This attribute describes the status of the requirement, for example, 'proposed', 'analyzed', 'deleted'.
Means of requirements validation	The intended means of validation of the requirement can be stated in this attribute, for example, 'review', 'simulation', 'study', 'demonstration'.
Requirements validation status	For instance 'to be validated', 'validated', 'not validated' (that is, validation failed in current state).
Requirements approval status	In some cases, some higher authority in the company needs to approve each requirement. Pre-defined values of this attribute may be 'to be approved', 'approved', 'not approved' (that is, approval not given in current state).
Means of design verification	The intended means of design verification against the requirement can be stated in this attribute, for example, 'review', 'simulation', 'study', 'demonstration'.
Design verification status	For instance 'to be verified', 'verified', 'not verified' (that is, design verification failed in current state).
Means of product verification	The intended means of product verification against the requirement can be stated in this attribute, for example, 'review', 'demonstration', 'test'.
Product verification status	For instance 'to be verified', 'verified', 'not verified' (that is, product verification failed in current state).
Allocation	The information regarding the proposed allocation of the requirement to another team or part of system architecture can be managed in this attribute.

In addition to these attributes, each requirement should be linked to its source if the source or reference information to the source is kept in the same requirements database. If not, the source attribute should be populated with the reference or a hyperlink to the source information.

A scenario describes an operational or other life cycle context, during which a system is required to show a specific behavior or have a specific characteristic or quality, whereas a use case describes one or several related and purposeful interactions between a human person or an external system (or element thereof) with the system of interest.

Exploring the different relevant scenarios and use cases during the development of a new system, usually as part of the requirements development process, helps to limit appropriately the validity of individual requirements, and contributes to ensuring the overall completeness of the requirements.

For example, a coast-guard surveillance aircraft system will have to operate in a number of operational scenarios, in each of which different things may be required. Similarly, the support personnel on ground will have certain use cases of how specific roles have to interact with the system, for example to refuel the aircraft or maintain it. It is important to know what the system is required to do in all relevant scenarios and use cases.

By applying both scenario and use case considerations to the development of requirements, significant benefits can be achieved: (1) certain requirements are cheaper to implement in the design of the system if they are only valid in particular scenarios or use cases, (2) the resulting set of requirements is more likely to be complete and (3) the identified scenarios and use cases will be helpful to plan and conduct the related V&V activities.

Traceability is key to being able to exploit the information that is generated and managed during the RM process. Traceability means the ability to trace related information objects such as sources of requirements, requirements and V&V data, for example by means of links or traceability matrices, in order to enable different types of analyses and the controlled reuse of these information objects.

Forward requirements traceability means the traceability from sources of requirements towards the resulting requirements. Backwards requirements traceability means the traceability from the requirements back to their sources.

Traceability can be further enriched by introducing different types of links and also relationships between several links.

In many cases, you will need a self-contained requirements document that is easily readable and understandable and that covers all necessary context information. The contained requirements should be structured in such a way within the requirements document that it facilitates a supplier's understanding of what is required. Table 5.14 offers a possible structure of a requirements document.

Table 5.14   A requirements document template

Chapter/sub-chapter	Comments
1. Context description	This first part of the document gives an overall introduction and addresses the intended context of the system to be developed at high-level.
1.1 Purpose of the system	High-level description of the overall purpose of the system to be developed.
1.2 Served system	This section of the document should contain a context diagram that identifies the boundaries of the served system, its components, actors, data flows, and so on.
1.3 Stakeholders	Including relevant stakeholder, domain experts, users, customers, clients, and so on.
1.4 Cultural and political aspects	Any particular aspects that have to be taken into account in general.
1.5 Strategy aspects	For example, a general preference to use COTS versus bespoke solution components.
1.6 Assumptions	High-level assumptions that are likely to have a major influence on the system development project/program, the system development process, or the system itself.
1.7 Open issues	Any significant open issues that have to be taken into account.
1.8 Glossary and definitions	The project/program terminology needs to be defined here to avoid misunderstandings.
2. Project/program constraints	This second part of the document addresses overall constraints on the project/program in terms of process requirements, that is, how the system has to be developed.
2.1 P&PM process requirements	How the project/program has to be managed.
2.2 SE process requirements	How the system has to be developed.
2.3 Procurement process requirements	How any procurement activities have to be conducted, for example regarding sub-components.
3. System requirements	This third part of the document addresses the requirements that the system itself has to satisfy, that is, what the system has to be able to deliver.

Table 5.14   *Concluded*

3.1 Scope of the system	Detailed definition of what exactly is in the scope of the system to be developed.
3.2 Operational scenarios	What are the operational scenarios in which the system is intended to be used?
3.3 Use cases	What are the use cases in which the system is intended to be used?
3.4 Functional tree	Representation of the identified functional tree, containing all functions that the system will have to fulfil in order to be used in its intended context.
3.5 Functional requirements	Derived from the functional tree and possibly allocations of functions to already known parts of the system's architecture.
3.6 Performance requirements	Specific performance aspects are addressed here, for example range or speed of the system.
3.7 Human machine interface (HMI) requirements	Human machine interfaces, formerly known as man machine interfaces (MMI), address the human user interfaces within systems, for example graphical user interfaces (GUIs).
3.8 Usability requirements	Specifying how the system has to be usable depending on the identified scenarios and use cases, and external circumstances.
3.9 Inter-operability requirements	Specifying how the system needs to be able to interact with other systems.
3.10 Interface requirements	Specific technical interface requirements in terms of geometrical, electric, mechanical, pneumatic, hydraulic, service, data or information, and process interfaces.
3.11 Cost requirements	Covering both non-recurring costs (for example, development related) and recurring costs (for example, production related) throughout the entire life cycle of the system.
3.12 Weight requirements	Addressing all weight requirements in all identified operational scenarios, including corresponding allowable weight limits, for example maximum take-off weight of an aircraft.
3.13 Maintainability requirements	Covering all relevant maintainability aspects of the system to be developed.
3.14 Data integrity requirements	In terms of data loss, data corruption and data theft.
3.15 Security requirements	All relevant security aspects the system has to incorporate are specified in this section.
3.16 Documentation requirements	Specifying how the system has to be documented, and how documentation has to be maintained throughout its life cycle.
3.17 Legal requirements	Any legal issues are addressed here as needed, for example safety or environmental protection related requirements such as the ban of certain materials or maximum noise levels.

A requirements document, that is, a set of requirements shall be:

- complete

- consistent

- non-redundant

- structured

- validated

- approved

All necessary requirements from all identified relevant stakeholders have to be present, and should have been analyzed. All defined categories of requirements should have been considered, and all identified scenarios, functions and use cases should have been taken into account.

No two requirements should be in direct conflict. Any such conflicts should have been identified, addressed and resolved by means of negotiation with the concerned relevant stakeholders. If this is not possible, the conflict has to be flagged up and a decision will have to be made at the relevant escalation level.

Each requirement should be expressed only once in the document or set of requirements. There should be no duplications, either full or partial duplications. Full duplications should lead to one of the duplicated requirements being deleted. Partial duplications are harder to spot and can often be resolved by combining concerned requirements.

There should be a clear structure within the requirements document. This structure can be based on one or several of the following criteria: system architecture, requirements type, work breakdown structure, project or program schedule, operational functions, system features, as well as identified scenarios and/or use cases. A good document structure is helpful because it facilitates the document's readability and analysis for completeness and consistency.

All requirements contained in the document have to be validated by the identified, relevant stakeholders. The owner or author of the document would have driven this validation process, and demonstrated to all relevant stakeholders that both at the individual requirements level and at the set of requirements level all quality criteria have been met. The formal validation confirms that the relevant stakeholders agree that the requirements are correct, consistent and complete.

In many cases, a designated manager or commercial representative will have to formally approve a requirements document. In such cases, the approver will have made sure that all quality criteria are met for the entire document before signing it off. Documents can also be approved in cases where not all requirements have been validated yet, for example to release a draft requirements document to a supplier or risk sharing partner. However, the contained requirements would be marked accordingly, that is, the validation status attribute would indicate that specific requirements have not been validated yet.

This workflow can be effectively enhanced by mind mapping, traceability establishment and analysis, as well as requirements quality analysis techniques. These should be supported by dedicated mind mapping or spreadsheet, object management, and requirements quality analysis tools.

RD workflow 3.5 – analyze and update requirements

This workflow is about analyzing and, if needed, updating the requirements that were newly written or reused, and structured into a comprehensive set during the previous workflow, in the light of the validated needs and their goal hierarchies.

The same quality criteria that were described previously and had to be applied when writing or reusing, and structuring the requirements are used again to ensure that the resulting requirements are of high quality.

This is important because it is easy to get carried away by the details of the requirements as you write them or compile them. Although the quality criteria should have already been observed when preparing the requirements, it is always good to check your work after you have done it.

It is also necessary to prepare the validation of the requirements by the relevant stakeholders. Being able to demonstrate to your relevant stakeholders that you have properly analyzed the requirements will facilitate the validation because it increases their confidence that the requirements are in fact of good quality. Table 5.15 displays the activities of this workflow, including their inputs and outputs, as well as the involvement of other participants.

The applicable quality criteria were described in the previous workflow, both at the individual requirement level and the set of requirements level. Appendices D and E provide a summary of these criteria.

When correcting any identified quality issues with the requirements, it is essential to resolve any conflicts with the concerned relevant stakeholders prior to entering the validation workflow. The last thing you want is having a large validation meeting with numerous stakeholders fighting about requirement conflicts they have only discovered during the meeting.

This workflow can be effectively enhanced by traceability analysis, requirements quality analysis and mind mapping techniques. These should be supported by dedicated object management, requirements quality analysis, and mind mapping or spreadsheet tools.

Table 5.15   Analyze and update requirements

Activity	Input	Output
Analyze each own requirement individually	Own requirements completed	Quality gaps of individual requirements identified
Update each own requirement as needed	Quality gaps of individual requirements identified	Own requirements updated individually
Analyze the complete set of own requirements	Own requirements updated individually	Conflicts and duplications identified
Resolve conflicts and duplications as needed with the concerned relevant stakeholders	Conflicts and duplications identified	All identified conflicts and duplications resolved
Update own requirements as needed	All identified conflicts and duplications resolved	Own requirements updated
Document the outcome of the analysis and the resolution of the identified conflicts and duplications	Own requirements updated	All updates documented

RD workflow 3.6 – validate requirements

This final workflow of the requirements development process is about obtaining the formal agreement of your relevant stakeholders that their identified needs are appropriately expressed in your set of requirements and that they consider the requirements to be of good quality in terms of their correctness, consistency and completeness.

This is important because all subsequent development work or purchasing efforts will be based on these validated requirements. Table 5.16 displays the activities of this workflow indicating the involvement of other participants, as well as the inputs and outputs of each activity.

All relevant stakeholders should be given the opportunity to look at the entire set of requirements prior to any validation meeting, not just at those of which they are directly the stakeholder. Traditionally, you would invite all relevant stakeholders to one formal meeting during which you would jointly go through the entire set of requirements, demonstrating the outcomes of your quality analyses if needed.

However, the validation can also be driven via video or telephone conference, or even via email. In some cases, especially in geographically dispersed teams, this may be the most economical way in the light of limited travel budgets. Still, in any case you have to be confident that the relevant stakeholders fully understand what you have done and agree with your outcomes, before they validate the requirements you have developed.

Table 5.16   Validate requirements

Activity	Input	Output
Prepare the validation of the requirements	Complete set of analyzed and updated own requirements	Relevant stakeholders invited to sessions
Drive the validation by the relevant stakeholders	Relevant stakeholders invited to sessions	Validation of requirements completed
Record the outcome of the validation	Validation of requirements completed	Outcome of requirements validation recorded
Implement any necessary changes	Changes necessary as agreed during the validation of requirements	Necessary changes implemented
Record the implementation of any necessary changes	Necessary changes implemented	Implemented changes recorded

All relevant stakeholders should validate those requirements for which they are the designated stakeholder only, but in the context of the other requirements within the set of requirements.

If you decide not to organize one stakeholder validation meeting, because it would take too long to find a suitable time slot for all concerned, or some of the relevant stakeholders are temporarily unavailable, you may prefer to drive the validation of your requirements with the relevant stakeholders individually, or in 'partial' validation meetings with only some of the relevant stakeholders participating at the time.

This workflow can be effectively enhanced by traceability analysis, requirements quality analysis, and mind mapping techniques – in terms of enabling the 'on demand' demonstration of evidence that sufficient analysis was carried out, and has led to updates of requirements as appropriate. These techniques have to be supported by object management, requirements quality analysis, and mind mapping or spreadsheet tools, so that the 'on demand' demonstration of evidence is possible.

Requirements Change Management

Once a new set of validated requirements has been established, this set needs to be kept up-to-date throughout the entire life cycle of the program, project, or system at hand. Step 4 of the RM process addresses this need.

There are many different factors for requirements change, both external and internal. For example, these might be changes in the market, in customer behavior or in their own business processes. Alternatively the company's internal production process might have changed, or new legislation was ratified that influences our required system characteristics.

Not being able to change our requirements in a flexible yet controlled and systematic manner would bear the risk of losing competitive advantage at best, or may even lead to project failure.

Therefore, a stringent change process has to be in place to enable systematic and controlled change of our requirements and also to avoid uncontrolled requirements creep and mutation. The importance of change impact analyses that are based upon the available traceability information cannot be emphasized too much.

A summary checklist of the entire RCM process is provided in Appendix C.

STEP 4 – MANAGE REQUIREMENTS CHANGE

The fourth step consists of the following six workflows: (1) 'Identify the need for change', (2) 'Analyze the impacts of the identified need for change', (3) 'Prepare the proposed change', (4) 'Analyze the impacts of the proposed change', (5) 'Agree the proposed change' and (6) 'Implement the agreed change'. The fifth workflow needs direct involvement of relevant stakeholders and domain experts, as marked in Figure 5.7.

RCM workflow 4.1 – identify the need for change

The first RCM workflow is about finding out that a requirements change is needed, or more accurately, whether a requirements change is needed. It is important that any such need be identified as soon as possible in order not to lose time, and to keep the costs that are caused by such a change as low as possible.

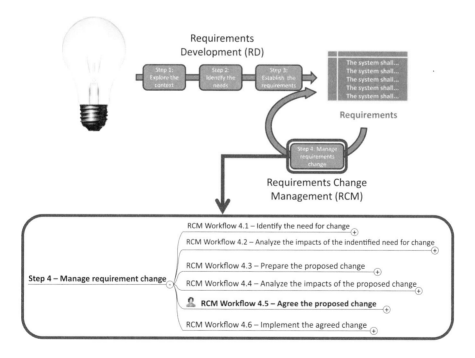

Figure 5.7   Manage requirements change

Not losing time is important for two main reasons. First, there are presumably people working on the basis of your requirements, for example finding and implementing a design solution that satisfies your requirements. If at least one of your requirements is wrong, that is, it needs to be changed, these people are working towards a partly wrong basis, thereby wasting time and money, until your requirements have been updated as appropriate.

Second, if it takes you a long time to update your requirements, this time will not be available for the recipients of your requirements to develop a new solution or find a new existing solution that satisfies your updated requirements. For example, this could mean that they may be forced to pick an existing, conventional solution due to the lack of time, instead of going for a more innovative solution that takes more time to develop. Table 5.17 displays the activities of this workflow, including their inputs and outputs.

You should make sure that you regularly check for any relevant requirements change notification from your relevant stakeholders or their organizations. This may be in the form of 'engineering change proposals' or 'requirement change notes', or in fact much less formal, with your customer sending you a letter that he wishes to make a change, depending on the specific context.

Also, within your own domain, you should keep your eyes open as to whether there are any changes in the domain knowledge or relevant regulation and legislation that may require changes of your requirements.

Table 5.17   Identify the need for change

Activity	Input	Output
Identify the need for change from the perspective of the relevant stakeholders	Requirement change notification received from relevant stakeholder	Need for change due to changes of input requirements identified
Identify the need for change from within the own domain	Update of relevant own domain knowledge	Need for change from within own domain identified
Identify the need for change due to changes of the relevant regulation or legislation	Relevant change of regulation or legislation	Need for change due to changes in regulation or legislation identified
Document the identified need for change	Need for change identified	Need for change documented

In any case, it is worthwhile keeping communication channels open with all identified relevant stakeholders and domain experts. Furthermore, automatic triggers could be put in place that allow you to be informed if certain events happen that may entail the need for change at your level. For instance, the last point could be realized by regularly scanning the reports of relevant change control board meetings whose outcomes may include changes of requirements that potentially have an impact on your area.

This workflow is greatly enhanced by traceability analysis techniques that are supported by an object management tool.

RCM workflow 4.2 – analyze the impacts of the identified need for change

The second RCM workflow is about identifying the likely impacts of the identified need for requirements change at your level. Impacted requirements have to be identified; and it has to be established whether any of these will have to be changed in order to be in line with the identified need for change. Any such need for change has to be categorized to be able to make sound decisions on where the change has to be addressed most urgently.

This workflow is important because it helps in providing a clear picture on the impacts of the identified need for change on your own level, that is, your requirements. It will help you to know which of your requirements are impacted by the identified need for change, which of them will have to be changed and how urgently, as well as of what type the expected changes of your requirements would be. Table 5.18 displays the activities of this workflow, including their inputs and outputs respectively.

Table 5.18   Analyze the impacts of the identified need for change

Activity	Input	Output
Identify which own requirements are impacted by the identified need for change	Need for change documented	Own requirements identified that are potentially impacted
Identify which own requirements will have to be changed	Own requirements identified that are potentially impacted	Own requirements identified that will have to be changed
Categorize the needed change of own requirements	Own requirements identified that will have to be changed	Needed changes to own requirements categorized
Document the outcome of the analysis	Needed changes to own requirements categorized	Outcome of impact analysis documented

Possible ways of how your impacted requirements may have to be changed in order to accommodate the identified change elsewhere are the following: modifying requirement statements, modifying the information contained in related requirement attributes, deleting existing links, creating new links, creating new requirements that are now needed, or deleting existing requirements that are no longer needed.

Whatever change of your impacted requirements is needed, it is good practice to keep a history of what was done, when, by whom and why. For example, if you decide that one of your existing requirements should be deleted in the light of an approved change proposal that will lead to a change of one of your input requirements, then your decision to delete your requirement should be documented with a reference to the underlying change proposal. This documented history information should just cover sufficient information, not in too much detail or the activity will soon keep you from doing your 'real' work.

Most commercial RM tools provide automatic history functionalities that track what information was entered, modified, deleted and linked, when and by which user, so that only reference information or other justification information needs to be entered manually.

Categories of the needed change of your own requirements could be expressed in terms of the urgency at which you have to respond to the underlying changes that are impacting your requirements; the severity of this impact; or the type of change that is needed.

This workflow can be effectively enhanced by traceability analysis and mind mapping techniques that should be supported by object management and mind mapping tools respectively.

RCM workflow 4.3 – prepare the proposed change

The next workflow is about preparing a proposed change of one or several of your requirements in response to the identified need for change, when applicable. This means that you should propose an update of your requirements, as you think it would best accommodate the identified need for change. This is important because you will have to get your stakeholders' 'buy-in'. They need to be happy with these changes, and will most probably have to formally agree with the changes you propose. Table 5.19 displays the activities of this workflow with their inputs and outputs.

After detailed consideration of all necessary changes to your requirements, you should prepare these changes in order to propose them to the relevant stakeholders, who will usually have to agree with your proposal before you can implement your proposed changes. In larger projects or programs, there will be a dedicated requirements change process in place, in which case you will have to apply this process in order to communicate your proposed changes of your own requirements.

The same quality criteria for 'writing good requirements' apply for any such proposed changes. It goes without saying that the proposed changes have to be analyzed in the light of the remaining set of requirements at your level. There is a great danger in updating some of your requirements, but no longer looking at the remaining set of requirements. The previously described analyses at both the individual requirement level and the set of requirements level have to be carried out again in the light of the proposed changes.

As with the previous workflow, this workflow can be effectively enhanced by traceability analysis and mind mapping techniques that are supported by object management and mind mapping tools.

Table 5.19   Prepare the proposed change

Activity	Input	Output
Formulate the proposed changes to own requirements	Outcome of impact analysis documented	Proposed changes to own requirements formulated
Complete the documentation and traceability of the proposed changes	Proposed changes to own requirements formulated	Proposed changes documented and traced

RCM workflow 4.4 – analyze the impacts of the proposed change

This workflow is about finding out what impacts the proposed changes of your requirements would have. This is important to know because if you wish your stakeholders to agree with your proposed changes they also need to know what impacts you expect these changes will have on the current situation. Such impacts may be related to system performance, project costs and/or schedule. Table 5.20 displays the activities of this workflow, as well as their inputs and outputs.

If a dedicated requirements change process was used to communicate the proposed change of your requirements, you will also receive feedback from the parties that are impacted by your proposed changes, that is, the recipients of your own requirements, be they internal or external to your organization. Any such feedback will be helpful in completing the picture with the expected budget and schedule implications of the proposed changes.

As with the two previous workflows, this workflow can be greatly enhanced by traceability analysis and mind mapping techniques that are supported by object management and mind mapping tools.

Table 5.20   Analyze the impacts of the proposed change

Activity	Input	Output
Analyze the impacts of the proposed changes internally	Proposed changes documented and traced	Impacts analyzed internally
Analyze the impact of the proposed changes externally	Proposed changes documented and traced	Impacts analyzed externally
Identify any relevant change process (if applicable)	Impacts analyzed internally and externally	Applicable change process identified
Document the outcome of the analysis	Applicable change process identified Change impacts analyzed	Outcome of impact analysis documented

RCM workflow 4.5 – agree the proposed changes

This workflow is about obtaining the agreement of your relevant stakeholders with the requirements changes that you propose. This agreement may be subject to a number of prior changes to your proposal. The outcomes of your change impact analysis from the previous workflow will help you to provide the relevant stakeholders with a good picture of what the proposed requirements change will entail. In fact, this agreement of the proposed changes by the relevant stakeholders corresponds to the validation described in the requirements development process.

The workflow is important because it will bring about the new requirements baseline. Table 5.21 displays the activities of this workflow including their inputs and outputs, and indicating the involvement of other participants.

Table 5.21   Agree the proposed changes

Activity	Input	Output
Prepare the validation of the proposed changes	Outcome of impact analysis documented	Relevant stakeholders invited to sessions
Drive the validation by the relevant stakeholders	Relevant stakeholders invited to sessions	Proposed changes to own requirements validated
Record the outcome of the validation	Proposed changes to own requirements validated	Outcome of validation documented
Implement any necessary changes	Outcome of validation documented	Necessary changes to the proposed changes implemented
Record the implementation of any necessary changes	Necessary changes to the proposed changes implemented	Implementation of necessary changes recorded

Traceability analysis, mind mapping, and presenting techniques are essential to facilitate this workflow. These techniques ought to be supported by dedicated object management, mind mapping and presentation tools.

RCM workflow 4.6 – implement the agreed changes

The last RCM workflow is about implementing the validated and agreed changes to your requirements in a controlled manner, and communicating them to the people that depend on your requirements, that is, the recipients of your requirements. These recipients will consider your requirements as their input requirements and they will have linked some of their own requirements to your requirements as the source or justification of their requirements. Alternatively they may have produced some design solution or product to meet your requirements.

Therefore it is important to communicate any changes you have implemented (without delay) to these recipients of your requirements. They need to know as early as possible what was changed and why, so that they can start in turn their own change process, as appropriate. Table 5.22 displays the activities of this workflow, including their inputs and outputs.

Table 5.22   Implement the agreed changes

Activity	Input	Output
Apply the agreed changes to own requirements	Changes to own requirements agreed	Agreed changes to own requirements applied
Check that the agreed changes to own requirements have been applied as agreed	Agreed changes to own requirements applied	Application of the agreed changes checked
Publish the new version of the requirements and trigger the relevant change process (if applicable)	Application of the agreed changes checked	Updated own requirements published Applicable change process triggered
Check that the underlying need for change has been met	Application of the agreed changes checked	Need satisfaction checked

This workflow can be greatly enhanced by traceability analysis, mind mapping, presenting, and reporting techniques. These should be supported by the appropriate object management, mind mapping, presentation and text editor tools respectively.

6

Techniques and Tools Supporting the RM Process

Chapter Summary

This chapter looks at a selection of techniques and tools, which support the RM process that was described in the previous chapter. In order to do so, we will first discuss the interaction with relevant stakeholders and domain experts, in particular regarding interviews and workshops, then we will introduce relevant techniques and tool categories in more detail. Finally, we will look at these techniques and tools from the viewpoints of the main functions within the RM process, that is, 'gathering and structuring information', 'tracing information', 'analyzing information', as well as 'reporting and documenting information'.

Interaction with Relevant Stakeholders and Domain Experts

Interactions with relevant stakeholders and domain experts, and in fact your own team members if any, are the key to success, because you depend on their knowledge and experience, as well as their willingness to share it with you openly. A lot of the relevant 'human' topics have been addressed in Chapter 4 in general.

There are two principal ways of interactively communicating with the people from whom you need to obtain relevant information – informal meetings, and more formal meetings, such as organized interviews and workshops. All of these can take place either face to face, by telephone, via the Internet including email, or by video conference.

If possible, especially until you know the people you are dealing with, face-to-face contact is preferable in general, but by no means essential, provided there is a certain amount of goodwill among the people you have to meet.

In any case, even more so in formal meetings, you should never waste other people's time, but carefully prepare and digest your meetings 'off-line'. People will notice that you are making an effort to use their precious time with respect and consideration. Hence, they will be more inclined to work with you, and they will spread the word, thereby creating powerful, positive word-of-mouth communications in your favor.

INTERVIEWS

Before inviting relevant stakeholders or domain experts to an interview, you should consider a number of things. First you should decide on the purpose of the interview. Following the RM process, you will normally know exactly what the purpose should be and you should have identified the people you need to speak to, that is, your relevant stakeholders and possibly other domain experts.

Based on the identified people you need to interview, their preferences, and their availability, you should decide whether you will conduct individual interviews or interviews with 2–3 people at the same time. You can find out about their preferences by simply giving them a call or sending an email, and about their availability by using the deployed email and scheduling tool, if you are working in the same company.

Also, you need to decide whether you will conduct a structured or unstructured interview to obtain the needed information. Think about how you may wish to visualize the things you are discussing, for example by means of a mock-up or other models or prototypes, and how you plan to record the interview, either by taking notes, or audio or video recording the meeting.

Then you should invite the interviewee(s) using the deployed email and scheduling tool. Try to select the most convenient place and time for the interviewee(s), not primarily thinking of yourself. In the meeting invitation, you should state the purpose of the meeting. Describe in just a few words what you are trying to achieve with their kind help, what you intend to address during the interview, how you plan to record any inputs from the interviewee(s), and what you intend to do with this information afterwards.

The meeting time should be between 30 minutes and a maximum of 2 hours, depending on what you have to cover, how many people are participating, and how available they are. Always be on time and well prepared. Never let your interviewee(s) wait for you.

There may be some occasions where the interviewee(s) insist on staying longer with you; but apart from these rare cases, make sure you always finish on time, or even earlier, if you have already covered everything. Also, do the information assessment 'off-line' following the meeting. Do not hold back the interviewee(s), while you go through what you have been recording.

WORKSHOPS

Workshops should be prepared in a similar way to interviews, only that the number of participants and the level of group dynamics are likely to be significantly higher. Workshops should be used with caution and only when really needed, because there is always the risk that extroverted, dominant participants will have the greatest influence on what information is exchanged and recorded, while introverted or shy personalities may find it difficult to come across with their information. Linked to the previous point, the average time that each participant will be used productively is much lower than is the case during an interview. So if a workshop is not managed well, and if there are many participants, some people may quickly have the impression that they are wasting their time. This is likely to lead to passive behavior during the workshop and, even worse, cause frustration among the participants.

Workshops, on the other hand, can be very effective when you actually need the interaction between the different participants in order to obtain the information and/or the agreement you require.

When preparing a workshop, try to find a quiet location, where the participants are least likely to be disturbed by their day-to-day business. Using a scribe who records the information obtained while you facilitate the workshop may be a good idea in some cases. Often, however, a scribe would not necessarily do as good a job of it as you can yourself, for example working with a mind map that can be seen and influenced by all as you go along.

Make sure you provide drinks and light food if possible, so that your participants will feel welcome and at ease during the workshop. This is often overlooked, but a worthwhile investment.

During the workshop, agree the intended purpose and methods. Very importantly, encourage constructive criticism, as well as free and open dialogue. Use feedback and information gained immediately 'on-line', or at least show what you record. Using a laptop and projector will allow you to enable this high level of interaction.

Techniques That Support the RM Process

There are many techniques available to support the RM process. In the previous section on the RM process, reference was made to relevant techniques for each process workflow. All of these techniques can be used in a complementary way. Most are based on or include some form of modeling. Some are based on the outcomes of the application of other techniques and/or will actually influence these outcomes. The following techniques have proven to be of both particular effectiveness and efficiency. However, this list is not exhaustive.

BRAINSTORMING

Brainstorming is a universal technique that can be applied in any context where you wish to collect within a group of people any available information that may potentially be relevant. Usually unstructured, each participant can 'throw in' any piece of information deemed potentially relevant. This information is immediately recorded and will not be discussed or rejected during the brainstorming itself. Following a brainstorming period of no longer than 5–15 minutes, the information captured can then be structured and assessed, confirmed as relevant, or rejected as irrelevant, and perhaps brought into a suitable format to be worked with subsequently.

MIND MAPPING

Mind mapping is an extremely powerful way of capturing and structuring information in an intuitive way. It allows you to share, discuss and update information, while interacting with relevant stakeholders and domain experts. This technique can also be used very effectively to support brainstorming sessions. Captured information can easily be structured or restructured following or even during the brainstorming session. Seemingly irrelevant inputs regarding topics or issues that are not addressed immediately can be kept in a 'waiting room' area of the mind map, for later consideration.

DIAGRAMMING USER INTERACTIONS

Diagramming user interactions is an essential technique as it allows the visualization of key aspects of the system to be developed, and its served system. A number of standards are available such as defined in the Unified Modeling Language (UML) and Systems Modeling Language (SysML). The most important items to be modeled are actors (persons, subsystems and so on) including external agents that are outside our control, use cases and scenarios, processes, data and communication flows, entity relationships, state transitions, and generally objects with their relationships.

FUNCTIONAL ANALYSIS

Functional analysis is about identifying the high-level functions of a system and breaking them down into a detailed functional tree across all levels of development or decomposition of the system. Different functions can then be allocated to relevant parts of the system architecture, and they will serve as the basis for the development of corresponding functional requirements for these parts. Also, the resulting functional tree will be used for additional analyses, such as certain safety analyses.

SAFETY ANALYSIS

Safety analysis comprises multiple safety relevant types of analysis, such as Particular Risk Analysis, Hazard Analysis and Fault Tree Analysis, which are often based on the identified functional tree. The main purpose of this technique is to identify what could go wrong with the new system and how it can be prevented from going wrong; thereby providing the basis for the development of safety requirements.

WHY-WHY-ANALYSIS

Why-why-analysis is universally applicable to any kind of problem for which we would like to identify the underlying causes in order to create relevant knowledge that can be used for the development of requirements which will contribute to prevent these problems from occurring.

SCENARIO ANALYSIS

Scenario analysis is about identifying all relevant scenarios that have to be considered for a new system, in particular but not exclusively its operational scenarios. This will help identifying exceptions, gaps, conditions and changes in priority regarding the identified requirements of a new system, and thereby it will help to increase the level of completeness, consistency and correctness of the requirements.

USE CASE ANALYSIS

Use case analysis consists of identifying, describing and evaluating all relevant cases of purposeful user interaction with and within the system of interest. These users can be human persons or external systems (or elements thereof).

In a given use case, a system may be required to show a specific behavior or have a specific characteristic or quality. During the use case analysis, it is very helpful to keep in mind the different scenarios and functions of the system that have already been identified.

Exploring the different relevant use cases during the development of a new system, in particular during the requirements elicitation, helps people not to forget important requirements, and to appropriately limit their validity to specific use cases as needed. Thereby this technique further helps to increase the level of completeness, consistency and correctness of the requirements.

WALKTHROUGH

Walkthrough is a very useful technique to review and improve workflows or business processes, thereby identifying constraints or functional requirements for a new system that is meant to be compatible with an existing business process. This technique consists of going or 'walking' through a business process or workflow of interest step by step, usually in a group of relevant domain experts, system users and system developers. While going through the process or workflow of interest, problems, issues, risks and opportunities may emerge and can be discussed by the participants, leading to the identification and an increased understanding of both constraints and requirements.

ESTABLISHING TRACEABILITY

Establishing traceability consists of creating meaningful links between relevant elements of the captured and structured information. Such links would normally be based on a defined 'business object model' or 'requirements data model', in which all classes and their relationships will be defined as they are intended to be captured and managed. Also, it comprises uniquely identifying each instance of such classes and capturing its versions and history. For example, each captured requirement in a team's requirements database should be of a certain format, contain the defined attributes including a unique identifier and have allowed links to the relevant input requirements. Furthermore, it should be possible to see which updated version of a requirement was created when, by whom, why, and what was changed.

TRACEABILITY ANALYSIS

Traceability analysis consists of using the established traceability between requirements across a number of development levels, as well as any associated data, such as V&V data, in order to know the status of the RM process, and how mature the requirements are. There are different types of traceability analysis, in particular 'impact analysis', which is essential during the requirements change process; 'derivation analysis', which provides insight into the extent to which requirements have been linked within the requirements cascade across several levels of development; and 'coverage analysis', which looks at the completeness of the expected links from one development level to the next, that is, within the requirements cascade [7].

REQUIREMENTS QUALITY ANALYSIS

Requirements quality analysis is about how individual requirements are expressed in terms of the textual requirement statement, and whether all required attribute information has been captured and appropriately recorded. Appendix D provides a requirements quality checklist for individual requirements that can be used in support of this technique.

PRESENTATION

Presentation is a universally important technique for most areas of business activities. In the context of RM it is used for different kinds of meetings in order to present RM relevant information that needs to be easily digested by the people participating in these meetings. Examples of such meetings may be project progress meetings, where the degree of completeness of the requirements across the cascade is shown.

REPORTING

Like the previous, this technique is universally important for most business areas. In the context of RM, it will be about creating relevant documents and written reports, such as requirements documents and validation meeting reports. The generation of Key Performance Indicators (KPIs) regarding the RM process is good practice. So-called 'dashboards' can be compiled from the measured KPIs on a regular basis, with the aim of visualizing key information on the current status, progress and trends.

Tools That Support the RM Process

Categorizing the tools that can be used to support the RM process via the above techniques is not straightforward, since most 'types of tools' are not mutually exclusive. In other words, the categories tend to overlap to a certain extent. Also, existing and well established example tools may fall into a number of categories. Nevertheless, it seems a good idea to think of the supporting tools in terms of the following categories, according to their main focus. Again, this list is not exhaustive.

SPREADSHEET TOOLS

Spreadsheet tools (example: Excel by Microsoft [27]) allow the capture, sorting, and ordering of data or information in columns and rows, plus their visualization in a large variety of ways, and for a wide range of purposes.

MIND MAPPING TOOLS

Mind mapping tools (example: MindManager by Mindjet [28], iMindMap by ThinkBuzan [29], and NovaMind by NovaMind [30]) support the creation and maintenance of mind maps, and offer a large variety of visual enhancements of the latter. Most mind mapping tools nowadays also provide links to commonly used scheduling, emailing, spreadsheet, presentation and text editor tools. Data can be exported from and imported into mind maps. These tools greatly support any meetings, such as workshops, in which information needs to be captured, structured, discussed, and restructured 'on-line', for example by using a projector, large screen or interactive white board during the meeting.

MODELING TOOLS

Modeling tools (example: MagicDraw by No Magic [31]) are based on the existing UML, SysML and other modeling standards, and they support the modeling of a large variety of items and their behaviors from multiple viewpoints. Examples of enabled diagrams are business process diagrams, entity relationship diagrams, state transitions diagrams, use case diagrams, context diagrams, and so on.

OBJECT MANAGEMENT TOOLS

Object management tools (example: DOORS by IBM [32], Cradle by 3SL [33] and RequisitePro by IBM [34]) serve to manage requirements as objects with multiple attributes and links to and from relevant associated data objects. The main advantage of these tools is that we can establish and use traceability within the requirements cascade across a number of development levels. Requirements are commonly treated as objects that are organized in modules, which represent requirements documents.

REQUIREMENTS QUALITY ANALYSIS TOOLS

There are many requirements quality analysis tools around (for example, Requirements Quality Analyzer by Re-use [35]) for a large variety of different types of analysis. The established requirements may be analyzed, for example, prior to their validation by using a requirements quality analysis tool that discovers weaknesses of the individual requirements. Based on the outcomes of such analyses, the individual requirements can be improved in terms of their correctness, consistency and completeness.

PRESENTATION TOOLS

Presentation tools (example: PowerPoint by Microsoft [27]) are used for different kinds of face-to-face or virtual meetings in order to present information that has to be easily digested by the participants. Depending mainly on the participants, it may sometimes be more efficient to work directly in the respective tool, such as the requirements database tool. However, if participants are not familiar with the deployed requirements database tool, the commonly used presentation tool will help to make them feel more at ease during the meeting.

TEXT EDITOR TOOLS

Text editor tools (example: Word by Microsoft [27]) are used to produce documents or written reports, such as requirements documents and validation meeting reports. In case a requirements database in a sophisticated RM tool is used, the 'working master' versions of the requirements will be in this database. When a document has to be produced, the requirements would be exported like a 'snapshot' from the database. If the requirements have to be updated, this would have to be done in the requirements database, not in the produced requirements document, and a new export would be carried out to produce the updated version of the requirements document, for example for the document to be formally signed.

The techniques and corresponding tool categories that were introduced above will be considered in the following sections under the headings of the main functions that are needed to support the RM process. These main functions are 'gathering and structuring information', 'tracing information', 'analyzing information', as well as 'reporting and documenting information'. For each of these main functions, the relevant techniques and tool categories will be provided, and their advantages and limitations discussed.

Gathering and Structuring Information

'Gathering and structuring information' is a key function to support the RM process. It is needed to elicit and capture the underlying domain knowledge that will be used to develop requirements. When you talk to relevant stakeholders and domain experts in order to find out about all relevant domains that you have to consider, you need to be able to capture any related information, visualize it, discuss it, structure it and keep it updated as needed when you talk with all other identified participants in the RM process.

Table 6.1 provides an overview of the main techniques that are of relevance in order to provide this function, as well as the tool categories that support these techniques. Advantages and limitations are proposed per technique and tool category from the perspective of the function 'gathering and structuring information'.

Table 6.1   Main techniques and tools (gathering and structuring information)

Technique	Advantages (+) and limitations (-)	Tool category	Advantages (+) and limitations (-)
Brainstorming	(+) very effective and efficient technique to gather unfiltered, initial information (−) captured information will have to be filtered for relevance, and structured or restructured following the brainstorming session	Mind mapping tools	(+) allow to capture very complex information of different degrees of granularity and detail, visualize it, and structure or restructure it
		Spreadsheet tools	(+) allow to capture information and visualize it (−) although structuring of information and subsequent ordering and restructuring is enabled, this is more difficult to achieve than with mind mapping tools
Mind mapping	(+) very effective and efficient technique to structure or restructure any information, extend it, link it, and visually enhance it with indicators or symbols (+) very suitable technique to confront additional participants at any moment with existing information, to receive and implement their feedback	Mind mapping tools	(+) greatly enhance the visualization of captured information, its traceability, its structuring and restructuring, as well as information updates over time
Diagramming user interactions	(+) very effective and efficient technique to elicit and capture or model the different, relevant aspects of the concerned domains (+) greatly supports the understanding of all relevant aspects of the 'served' system and context, the 'as is' system and the 'to be' system	Modeling tools	(+) provide the capability to use the various notations to model the information captured from a multitude of different viewpoints (+) impact analysis of any changes of the content and structure of the information is well supported (−) in-depth knowledge of the used notation(s) is necessary and takes time to acquire

Table 6.1   *Concluded*

Functional analysis	(+) allows to elicit and capture the functions of a system, and subsequently break them down into a functional tree (+) creates the basis for the development of functional system requirements and a number of other analyses such as safety analysis (−) cannot be completed in isolation from the system architecture development, since lower level functions in the tree will have to be allocated to architecture components and elements	Modeling tools	(+) support the creation of detailed functional models that can be linked to other, architecture related models (+) support comprehensive considerations and updates of the created functional and architecture models
		Mind mapping tools	(+) easy and quick to use (−) limited capability to visualize complex models
		Spreadsheet tools	(+) easy and quick to use (−) limited capability to visualize complex models
Safety analysis	(+) create the basis for the development of safety related requirements at all levels of development (−) are dependent on both the functional tree and the system architecture across all development levels	Modeling tools	(+) support the capture of complex information
		Mind mapping tools	(+) easy and quick to use (−) limited capability to visualize complex models
		Spreadsheet tools	(+) easy and quick to use (−) limited capability to visualize complex models
Why-why analysis	(+) generic technique to identify root causes of problems or risks	Mind mapping tools	(+) easy and quick to use
		Spreadsheet tools	(+) easy and quick to use
Scenario analysis	(+) helpful to identify all needed system functions, scenario dependent system properties, and conditions for specific requirements	Modeling tools	(+) support the capture of complex information
		Mind mapping tools	(+) easy and quick to use
		Spreadsheet tools	(+) easy and quick to use
Use case analysis	(+) allows to identify and capture the relevant user interactions with the system of interest (+) contributes to the completeness, consistency and correctness of the requirements (−) cannot be completed in isolation from the system architecture development and has to be based on scenario and functional considerations	Modeling tools	(+) support the creation of detailed use case and interaction related models that can be linked to relevant other models (+) support comprehensive considerations and updates of the created models
		Mind mapping tools	(+) easy and quick to use (−) limited capability to visualize complex models
		Spreadsheet tools	(+) easy and quick to use (−) limited capability to visualize complex models
Walkthrough	(+) helpful to complete the elicitation and capture of relevant business process information, trigger participant interaction, and avoid misunderstandings	Modeling tools	(+) support the capture of complex information
		Mind mapping tools	(+) easy and quick to use
		Spreadsheet tools	(+) easy and quick to use

Tracing Information

'Tracing information' is another key function to support the RM process, insofar as we always need to be able to know where specific information has come from, and what new information was created based on the captured information. Also, there will usually be many changes during the life cycle of a system; and we need to be able to analyze impacts of these changes, or proposed changes. Impacts have to be analyzed thoroughly so that we know what else will have to be changed as a consequence, how long it will take, using how many resources, and how much it will cost us in the end.

Without traceability in place, it is very cumbersome or – in more complex environments – even impossible to do this in an appropriate manner. For example, the change of a requirement during the development of a system may have impacts on a number of other requirements at the level below in the extended enterprise. We need to know what these impacts are, including cost, schedule and risk implications, in order to make the right decision on whether or not to accept this change (provided we have a choice). Furthermore, we can make emerging risks or expected non-compliances and their impacts explicit.

Table 6.2 provides an overview of the main techniques that are of relevance in order to provide this function, as well as the tool categories that support these techniques. Advantages and limitations are proposed per technique and tool category from the perspective of the function 'tracing information'.

Table 6.2   Main techniques and tools (tracing information)

Technique	Advantages (+) and limitations (−)	Tool category	Advantages (+) and limitations (−)
Establishing traceability	(+) forms the essential basis for any subsequent traceability analyses (+) enables efficient reuse of the captured information (+) enables monitoring and controlling the RM process (+) essential basis for the initial validation and subsequent change management of requirements	Object management tools	(+) facilitate the creation and follow up of links (+) automatically create and store unique object identifiers; as well as versioning and authoring information (+) support traceability of very complex information (−) it is necessary to define a suitable business object model or a requirements data model that can be used to filter, sort and identify all managed objects and their relationships
		Mind mapping tools	(+) links are enabled (−) links are difficult to create and to follow up (−) not manageable with large numbers of objects
		Spreadsheet tools	(+) links are supported via matrices in spreadsheets (−) links are difficult to create and to follow up (−) not manageable with large numbers of objects

Analyzing Information

'Analyzing information' is the third essential function to support the RM process. It is based on captured and traced information, and helps measuring and controlling the RM process. Weaknesses can be identified and addressed regarding traceability itself, individual requirements, and sets of requirements in order to improve the quality of the requirements and their traceability to any associated objects.

Table 6.3 provides an overview of the main techniques that are of relevance in order to provide this function, as well as the categories of tools that support these techniques. Advantages and limitations are proposed per technique and tool category from the perspective of the function 'analyzing information'.

Table 6.3   Main techniques and tools (analyzing information)

Technique	Advantages (+) and limitations (−)	Tool category	Advantages (+) and limitations (−)
Traceability analysis	(+) provides valuable insights regarding the status of the RM process and linked V&V activities across the extended enterprise (+) supports change management processes (−) relies on high quality linking in order to be effective (if the links are wrong, the outcomes will be wrong as well)	Object management tools	(+) enable object and traceability management over time and across levels (+) enable manual filtering, sorting, reviewing of linked objects in definable views based on the deployed requirements data model
		Mind mapping tools	(−) support only manual browsing of traceability (−) are limited to small numbers of objects/levels
		Spreadsheet tools	(+) support filtering and sorting of linked objects (−) are limited to small numbers of objects/levels
Requirements quality analysis	(+) helps to improve the quality of individual requirements in terms of their completeness and correctness (that is, statement, attributes and links) (−) is usually applied after the requirements have been written, not during the process of writing them (−) requires the underlying RM data model and dictionaries to be of good quality (−) does not investigate the completeness and consistency of entire sets of requirements	Requirements quality analysis tools	(+) enable analysis of large numbers of objects/levels (+) provide automatic checking and reporting against defined dictionaries and rules (−) still require human interpretation of the findings (−) are of use only once the requirements have been written
		Object management tools	(−) support only manual checks of objects via filtering, sorting and views (−) are limited to small numbers of objects/levels
		Spreadsheet tools	(−) support only manual checks of objects via filtering, sorting and views (−) are limited to small numbers of objects/ levels

Reporting and Documenting Information

'Reporting and documenting information' is the fourth key function to support the RM process. All of the above techniques will lead to outputs – potentially from a number of supporting tools – that will have to be reported, documented and presented in some way. Sometimes the respective tool environment could be used to present the relevant information, but it seems to be accepted practice across many sectors to produce presentations and documents. These will be shared either face to face, in virtual meetings, by email and/or stored in some document management system.

The business environment in which the RM process is applied will usually have a pre-defined way of how and in which format and frequency these things will have to be done. Reporting and documenting is important from the RM viewpoint because this helps in communicating to all stakeholders and controlling the RM process.

Table 6.4 provides an overview of the main techniques that are of relevance in order to provide this function, as well as the categories of tools that support these techniques. Advantages and limitations are proposed per technique and tool category from the perspective of the function 'reporting and documenting information'.

Appendix G provides a detailed mapping of the RM process workflows that were described in Chapter 5 to the recommended techniques and types of tools that were the focus of this chapter.

Table 6.4   Main techniques and tools (reporting and documenting information)

Technique	Advantages (+) and limitations (−)	Tool category	Advantages (+) and limitations (−)
Presenting	(+) information can be communicated at the right level of detail and granularity for the intended public (relevant stakeholders or domain experts) and without confronting the public with the 'look and feel' of the multiple RM tools used (−) additional work is required to prepare visualizations of information that is managed in specific RM tools	Presentation tools	(+) provide usually a high degree of compatibility among the different tools that are used in support of the RM process (+) are usually highly sophisticated and mature (being deployed across many industries and private households worldwide)
Reporting	(+) helps to provide detailed documentation of all relevant aspects of RM (+) enables controlling and justification of the RM process and the overall project/program (−) additional work is required to prepare documentation of information that is managed in specific RM tools	Text editor tools	(+) provide usually a high degree of compatibility among the different tools that are used in support of the RM process (+) are usually highly sophisticated and mature (being deployed across many industries and private households worldwide)

7

The Use of RM at Three Levels of System Complexity

Chapter Summary

This chapter addresses the application of RM at different levels of system complexity, and provides detailed and graphical insights into three representative example cases. It will help you understand in what category of context you are yourself, and therefore allow you to select the appropriate level of detail and formalism of the RM approach that you should apply in your specific circumstances.

Three Levels of System Complexity

The three levels of system complexity described and exemplified in this chapter are not clear-cut categories. They merely serve the purpose of allowing you to decide for yourself whether you consider the system you have to deal with in your own context to be 'simple', 'complex' or 'highly complex'. This will give you an indication of which degree of formality and detail your RM approach should be and, based on this, which methods and supporting tools you should use to develop your requirements, and manage them over time.

In the following sections, all three levels of system complexity will be described by giving a number of example systems that can be argued to fall into each category, the typical characteristics of related projects that are needed to develop such systems, the human resources needed to develop and manage the requirements for these projects, the recommended RM tooling, and some general practical advice.

Then, in order to illustrate all three categories, a more detailed example case will be provided for each level of system complexity, that is, an organized trip to New York for students of a British university, a school development project in the Democratic Republic of the Congo, and the global Airbus A350 XWB (eXtra Wide Body) aircraft program, respectively.

Simple Systems (Level 1)

As introduced before, systems can be defined as integrated sets of interacting elements, such as products, services, people, processes, hardware, software, firmware and information, that serve a defined purpose. All systems are inherently not really 'simple' in absolute terms, so that the adjective 'simple' here has to be seen as relative to other more complex types of systems.

Figure 7.1 provides a number of examples and typical characteristics of simple systems. Examples for this category of systems could be a new house, a journey, a charity organization, or a new family car. Depending on the individual circumstances, these systems would usually be purchased or there may also be some personal involvement. For instance, you may want to plan your trip alone, or outsource this work to your travel agent. Also, you may wish to design your new house and do a lot of the work yourself, or you may contract an architect who does it for you.

Whatever your solution will be in the end, you should first develop your requirements. This way, you are able to make the right decisions and follow up the successful completion or purchase of the system, that is, check that all your requirements are satisfied, and if not, find out why, and if this is acceptable for you in your specific situation.

Typical characteristics of the needed projects to put in place this type of systems would be the following: the duration of such projects could be anything from a day to several years. The budget may be from $100.00 for a weekend trip, to several million dollars for a large house.

Risks may usually be relatively low if the integrated system is purchased from a professional organization that integrates and delivers the system for you. Often it is much riskier if you do part of the work yourself without having the necessary skills or experience, for example if you intend to install the plumbing and electrics in your newly built house yourself without having any experience in this domain in order to save money.

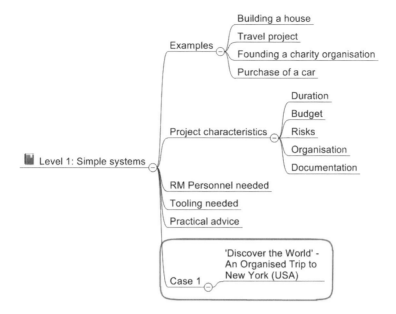

Figure 7.1   Use of RM for simple systems

The organization may consist only of you, or a small number of key-actors such as the car salesman, the house architect or the tax consultant. The documentation may consist of your list of requirements, a number of sales brochures on alternative solutions, as well as any required legal documents and/or contracts.

Regarding the RM resources needed, you would probably be doing this work by yourself, using anything from a sheet of paper, via electronic spreadsheets, to a mind mapping tool, in order to manage the information you need for the development and maintenance of your requirements.

Some practical and very obvious advice would be to try to avoid the trap of not taking the time to develop your requirements. This will only take little time, as it does not need to be formal, and you can use simple tools. But if you do not know what you really need, the chances are that you will probably not buy or make what you need.

EXAMPLE CASE 1:'DISCOVER THE WORLD' – AN ORGANIZED TRIP TO NEW YORK (USA)

A British university with a high percentage of global students, mainly coming from continental Europe, Africa and Asia, decided on a strategy to improve the perceived attractiveness of their institution among potential students worldwide. At the same time, the university aimed to enhance some of the taught subjects in their key faculties, in particular Arts, Theology, Music, Sports, Social Sciences, Environment and Civil Engineering, and effectively improve their brand image in their international target market segments.

The decision was made to develop and institutionalize a multidisciplinary yearly study trip that could be exploited for the university's marketing purposes, while significantly enhancing the quality of some of the courses offered to students.

During an initial brainstorming workshop with leading staff members of the concerned faculties and the dean of the university, a number of relevant topics were identified that needed to be explored in more detail. Two main decisions were made at the end of this meeting: the destination of the study trip in question should be New York (Figure 7.2), and a member of the Social

Figure 7.2   More than the Statue of Liberty

Sciences faculty volunteered to act as the interim project manager and take the necessary steps for the preparation of a detailed 'kick-off' meeting a few weeks later.

The former decision was made because New York was perceived by all present as the most 'international' city in the world, offering a large variety of all types of activities that could be of interest for such a trip. The latter decision was made because the interim project manager had some experience in applied action research and project management in the context of several United Nations development projects in Africa.

Figure 7.3 provides an overview of the main stakeholders in the institutionalized trip, that is, the 'system', and their respective needs. The

Figure 7.3   The main stakeholders and their needs

identified stakeholders were the university, the US Homeland Security, the university's students union, involved students, involved teaching staff members, and students' parents and families.

The identified needs of the university were the following. First, the university needed a responsible focal point in place, that is, a suitable project manager who develops and conducts the trip for the first time, and subsequently keeps the system up to date and under control. Second, the university needed to comply with all applicable policies and regulations, in particular the university's health and safety, equal opportunities and travel policies. Third, the teaching schedule at the university needed to be respected. Fourth, the university needed to exploit the system for their advertisement and marketing activities, while offering a variety of attractive activities to their students that enhance their teaching experience. Fifth, the activities offered as part of the system needed to be of direct relevance for the taught subjects in the above-mentioned faculties of the university. And finally, the system needed to avoid any direct costs to the university, that is, only the indirect cost of keeping the system up to date and under control should be incurred by the university, not any direct travel expenses for the trip.

These stakeholder needs led to a number of more specific goals and, based on these, to a set of detailed requirements that had to be satisfied by the system. In other words, the necessary organization of the trip had to make sure that all requirements were addressed and met, where possible. If a requirement could not be met, then a decision could be made as to whether this fact was acceptable or not. This way, any non-compliances could be made visible, and necessary changes to the system initiated.

In order to satisfy the academic requirements, subject relevant activities were integrated into the trip in order to enhance the perceived teaching experience of the participating students in the respective subjects (Figure 7.4).

Concerning religious studies, for instance, a number of attendances in worship sessions that were followed by explanatory sessions were organized in different communities: the Roman Catholic St. Peter's Church next to Ground Zero, which belongs to the oldest Catholic parish in New York; the inter-denominational Times Square Church that uses a former theatre building and enjoys an international gospel choir with a worldwide reputation; the Central Synagogue near Central Park that serves as a vibrant Jewish community center; and the Islamic Cultural Center of New York, which comprises the first mosque that was built in the city and hosts a large variety of Islamic community events.

Figure 7.4   Meeting the academic requirements

Regarding civil engineering, a special visit to the 9/11 Memorial and the construction site of the New World Trade Center buildings was organized, with leading civil engineering experts giving the students in-depth explanations about their remarkable work, and the many challenges they were facing.

Finally, a number of world-class art museums were visited, such as the Metropolitan Museum of Art including the Cloisters, the Museum of Modern Art, and a number of private, contemporary art galleries in mid-town Manhattan.

Complex Systems (Level 2)

Figure 7.5 provides a number of examples and typical project characteristics of complex systems. Examples for this category of systems could be a new school, a water distribution system for a small village, a website for an e-commerce company, or training modules for the flight crews of a major airline. This type of system would usually be developed and deployed by dedicated organizations, either within a project or a program.

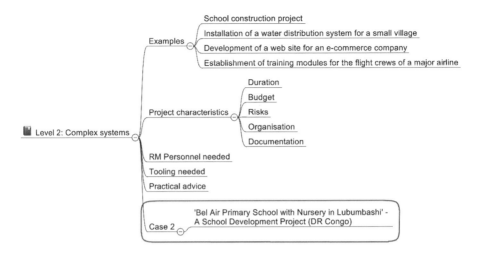

Figure 7.5   Use of RM for complex systems

Typical characteristics of the needed projects to realize this type of system could be the following. The duration of such projects may be from several months to several years. The necessary budget may be from several thousand US dollars to several million dollars. Risks have to be managed effectively throughout such projects.

The documentation will consist of a set of formal project and system documents including detailed user manuals or similar. There are also likely to be legal requirements in place that both the project and the system will have to comply with.

Regarding the RM resources needed, a professional requirements manager should be appointed, who would develop the project and system requirements and manage them over time, using sophisticated RM tools such as a mind mapping tool and a requirements database.

Some practical advice would be to make sure that the requirements manager is appointed as early as possible in the process of establishing the project that will develop the system in question. The effective management of project and system requirements is key for any project to be successful. Without them, we do not really know what the project is exactly about, and we are likely to work away into a wrong direction. Unfortunately, there are many examples where the requirements manager joins the project team quite late into a project.

Ideally, we should have the initial high-level requirements established before we even take the decision to launch a project.

EXAMPLE CASE 2: 'BEL AIR PRIMARY SCHOOL WITH NURSERY IN LUBUMBASHI' – A SCHOOL DEVELOPMENT PROJECT (DR CONGO)

The Bel Air school construction project in Lubumbashi was initially decided in October 2007 in the light of the urgent need to offer schooling to children of the Bel Air district of the second largest town of the Democratic Republic of the Congo (after the capital Kinshasa). In this part of Lubumbashi with its more than 60,000 inhabitants, 65 per cent of whom are children, there were no proper schools available that could take in pupils from this very poor area of the town. The fact that the population of this part of Lubumbashi was increasing at a dramatic rate made the need even more urgent.

The Salvatorians (Society of the Divine Saviour) are a Roman Catholic religious order that operate globally. Salvatorian priests, sisters and brothers in the Katanga province of the Democratic Republic of the Congo were already running a number of nurseries, primary schools and secondary schools in the region, and planned the construction of additional schools.

The Salvatorian novitiate in the Bel Air district was large enough to enclose the new primary school and nursery, and offer school children a protected learning environment, as well as pastoral care. In particular, children from very poor living conditions would be given the opportunity to learn and have a good start in life, based on faith, love and honesty.

The nursery was to comprise 6 classes with up to 35 children per class, for children of 3 to 6 years of age, whereas the primary school would eventually include 16 classes with up to 45 children per class, for children of 7 to 12 years of age.

With the financial support of the Salvatorian Office for International Aid (SOFIA) [36] and a number of other private charity projects and donors, the construction could begin in 2010 (Figure 7.6), starting with the needed sanitary facilities, that is, toilets, showers and washrooms, followed by administration rooms, the assembly hall and the first classrooms for the nursery. The nursery was completed in May 2011. Teachers were recruited and the nursery opened its doors in September 2011. Since then, the focus has been on the construction of the needed primary school classrooms.

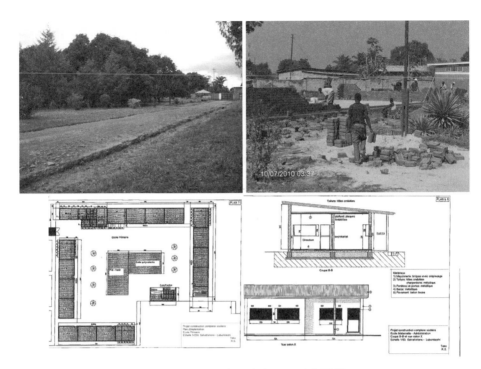

Figure 7.6   Starting the construction (Photos: SOFIA)

One of the most challenging issues was found to be the establishment and management of the donors' requirements, that is, the specific requirements of the supporting institutions and private donors. Many constraints and conditions are usually linked to the use of such donations for development projects.

Finding out what these requirements are is essential because the entire funding of the project depends on it. Examples of types of donor requirements are reporting requirements (many donors have their own ideas about how they want to receive feedback on the progress made), and project constraints that are necessary to qualify for a specific governmental or institutional funding scheme, in other words conditions that have to be met by the project in order to successfully apply for funding.

The school is not only about the building, of course; rather it has to be seen as a complex system that needed to be realized via a project that was concerned with both the construction of the school and the establishment of stable school operations. Figure 7.7 provides an overview of the main project stakeholders and their needs.

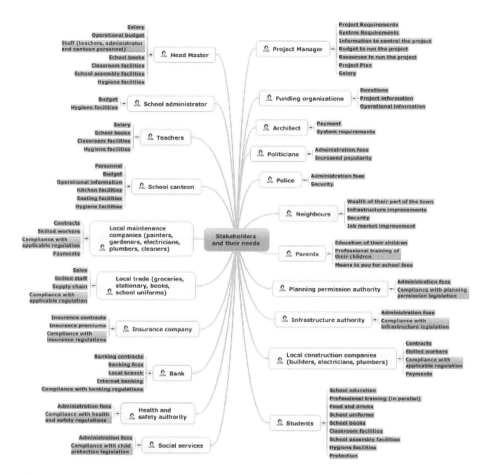

Figure 7.7   The main stakeholders and their needs

Requirements regarding both the construction of the school and the subsequent establishment of school operations had to be developed based on the analyzed needs of the main project stakeholders. This included reporting requirements and certain constraints on the overall project in order to qualify for the financial support by particular institutions and private donors. Any conflicts between resulting requirements, for instance regarding the schedule or budget of the project, had to be negotiated and resolved with the concerned stakeholders.

If certain requirements could not be met, because fewer donations were received than expected or bad weather hindered progress, this did not lead to an automatic deletion of these requirements. What was required was still required. Rather any forms of non-compliance or associated risks had to be systematically identified and managed, based on the validated requirements.

Also, the priority of requirements could change over time. For example, if new health and safety legislation were implemented, this would potentially lead to new or modified requirements, or possibly to a change of the priorities of the requirements during the project. All requirements had to be kept up to date over time, so that if any such changes occurred and had an impact on the requirements, this very fact could be systematically recorded and addressed in the appropriate manner.

This school development project represents a significant and sustainable contribution to the many generations of children who will benefit from this school, their families, local businesses and trade, as well as the entire local community (Figure 7.8).

Figure 7.8   Completing the school (Photos: SOFIA)

Highly Complex Systems (Level 3)

Figure 7.9 provides a number of examples and typical characteristics of highly complex systems. Examples for this category of systems could be a new aircraft, a passenger car, the merger of a banking company, or a regional renewable energy system. As in the case of complex systems, this type of system would be developed and deployed by dedicated program and/or project organizations.

Typical characteristics of the necessary projects to realize this type of system could be the following. The duration of such projects may be from one to several years. The needed budget will probably range from several million US dollars to several billion dollars.

All aspects of P&PM, including risk and opportunity management as well as SE, have to be conducted by highly skilled and experienced professional team members. The organization in place to realize such systems will probably range from several hundred to several thousand employees within the extended enterprise, and is likely to be geographically dispersed globally.

The documentation will consist of large sets of formal project, program and system documents including contracts and detailed in-service support documentation at all development levels of the extended enterprise.

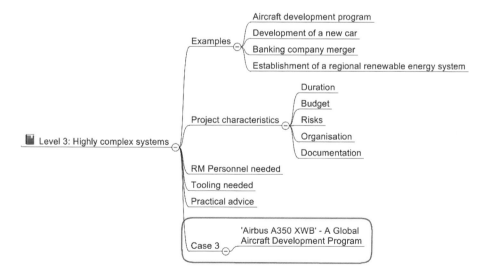

Figure 7.9   Use of RM for highly complex systems

Regarding the RM resources needed, professional requirements managers have to be appointed for each major development team within the extended enterprise. This network of requirements managers should cooperate closely across all levels of the extended enterprise, using the same RM standards, the same core RM data model, and sophisticated tools that are compatible throughout the extended enterprise.

Some practical advice would be to make sure that at the program or project level, the requirements manager is appointed as early as possible during the process of establishing the project or program – for the same reasons mentioned before (regarding complex systems).

EXAMPLE CASE 3: 'AIRBUS A350 XWB' – A GLOBAL AIRCRAFT DEVELOPMENT PROGRAM

Within Airbus [37], the A350 XWB program is the second aircraft development program after the A400M program that fully deployed RM supported by the commercial DOORS software tool. Based on the experience made with the RM deployment for the military A400M program, this RM deployment had reached a very high level of maturity, and was rolled out early from the beginning of the A350 XWB program.

The DOORS tool was originally developed and marketed by the IT company Telelogic, which was taken over by IBM a few years into the program. The add-on tool RMF (Requirements Management Framework) was deployed in addition to the standard DOORS tool, offering new functionalities, in particular regarding the Configuration Management of individual requirements.

The A350 XWB program (Figure 7.10) has come to run the largest DOORS requirements database within the EADS concern – and probably worldwide – with over 3,500 users in six countries, that is, France, Germany, UK, Spain, USA and India. The central DOORS servers are based in Toulouse, France.

Figure 7.10   The Airbus A350 XWB (Photo: Airbus)

In order to exchange requirements and their associated V&V data between different teams in the global extended enterprise (Figure 7.11), an additional tool called 'Data Exchange' was used. This technical solution allowed the exchange of data between different DOORS databases of compatible major versions of the DOORS tool.

The main advantage of exchanging requirements modules including V&V data between Airbus, Risk Sharing Partners and suppliers was that on both sides traceability could be established to those requirements that were under the control of the other side respectively.

For instance, in the Airbus requirements database, supplier requirements modules were mirrored, which allowed for far greater visibility into how the suppliers have further broken down the requirements within their own company, and how their design actually met the applicable requirements; that is, the Design Verification status could be assessed at Airbus even for lower development levels. This helped to reduce risks and gain confidence in the progress of the development work outside Airbus.

Main challenges of this way of working in the global extended enterprise of the A350 XWB program were the user and access rights management; ongoing enhancement projects on the DOORS tooling, such as script developments or the implementation of new tool functionalities; and keeping the tool environment up and running at high performance, across a number of different countries and time zones, while ensuring data protection in terms of data security and integrity.

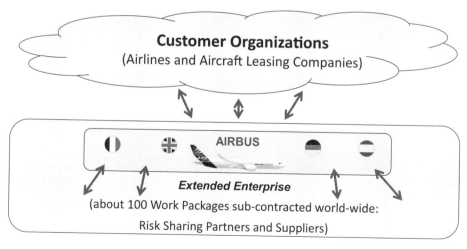

Figure 7.11   **The extended enterprise of the A350 XWB program**

Within the A350 XWB program, Airbus subcontracted around 100 major work packages globally, to both Risk Sharing Partners and traditional suppliers. Usually, these major work packages were to a large extent further subcontracted to a high number of other suppliers, thereby forming an immense, global 'supply network'. The work contracted out to this 'supply network' represents a substantial percentage of the overall development and production work of the program. All these work packages were specified and driven by requirements.

Overall, the A350 XWB program and all related development work was driven by several hundred thousand requirements that were organized across a number of levels within Airbus from the program level, via the aircraft level, the component level, the sub-assembly level to the work package level. These work packages were in many cases broken down further into several more detailed levels within the extended enterprise. This organization of the A350 XWB requirements is called the A350 XWB requirements cascade.

Figure 7.12 offers a simplified overview of the requirements cascade of the A350 XWB program. The cascade shown is simplified insofar as it does only show the schematic organization of requirements modules within the requirements database. Each such module represents a requirements document, that is, a set of structured individual requirements that belong together, in order to specify some specific aspect of the A350 XWB program. Individual requirements in each of these modules are linked to one or several individual requirements in other modules.

For example, one given requirement at any level would usually be linked to its input requirement(s), normally at the level above, and some requirements at the level below would usually be linked to it in a similar way. Through this traceability, one can easily follow up where individual requirements come from, across all levels of the cascade.

Furthermore, the cascade is simplified insofar as it does not show any other modules that are associated with the requirements modules, for example modules containing Requirements Validation data or Design Verification data that are linked to individual requirements. These links between requirements and V&V data allow to plan suitable V&V activities regarding each requirement in the cascade, and to follow up the V&V status of each requirement during the development life cycle.

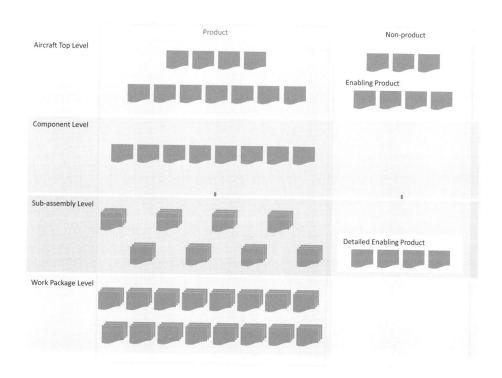

Figure 7.12   The simplified A350 XWB requirements cascade

Finally, the distinction was made between product and non-product requirements. The former were concerned with the A350 XWB aircraft itself, that is, the primary system to be developed in this program, whereas the latter were concerned with how the A350 XWB aircraft was to be developed, produced and supported in service.

Non-product requirements specified the processes and types of organization that had to be put in place, as well as any regulation that had to be complied with, in order to develop the aircraft. Part of the non-product requirements specified the 'enabling product' that had to be developed and produced in parallel, so that it was ready in time for the ramp-up of the series aircraft production. This enabling product consisted among other things of the industrial system – including manufacturing facilities, the transportation system for equipped intermediate components, the final assembly lines and testing facilities, as well as the aircraft delivery centers.

8

Conclusion

To summarize, this book addressed a wide range of key aspects of Requirements Management (RM) in the context of both Systems Engineering (SE) and Project and Program Management (P&PM) – and proposed a generic RM process that is knowledge-driven and enables the successful development and maintenance of program, project and system requirements in complex business environments.

The first part of the book introduced important aspects of RM and the context in which RM helps to run successful programs and projects. Chapter 1 offered an introduction to the book, including guidance on how to use this book most effectively and efficiently, as well as an introduction to RM itself as a discipline, and why requirements and RM are so crucial for the successful completion of projects.

Chapters 2 and 3 put RM into the context of SE and P&PM respectively, defining what is understood by each, why they are so important and what role RM plays in both contexts.

The second part of the book dealt with how RM can be put into practice. Chapter 4 addressed some key human factors that are essential to successfully deploy a new RM process in any organization. Chapter 5 provided a detailed description of all aspects of the proposed RM process, followed in Chapter 6 by the description of RM techniques and types of tools that support this process.

Although these three chapters were written in generic terms, the underlying assumption was that the RM process was to be applied for the development of complex or highly complex systems. This means that for simple systems, many of the proposed activities would be much less time-consuming, and the needed tooling to support the process and manage the created data would not have to be so sophisticated. This is mainly so because for simple systems the data volumes are usually significantly lower.

Finally, Chapter 7 explored the application of RM at different levels of system complexity, and provided detailed and graphical insights into three representative example cases. Thereby it will have been of help to better understand in what category of context you are yourself, and select the appropriate level of detail and formalism of the RM approach that you should apply in your specific circumstances.

Throughout the book, references were made to the detailed appendices provided, including human aspects (Dos and Don'ts), RM process checklists for both requirements development (RD) and requirements change management (RCM), a list of recommended RM tools, a requirements quality checklist, a requirements document quality checklist, as well as a mapping of the RM process workflows to the recommended techniques and types of tools that can best support them.

Whatever your background, experience and business purpose, this book offers you flexible advice and guidance in terms of RM, depending on your own individual needs. If you have just started working as a requirements manager, you might wish to apply the proposed approach in its entirety to your working context. If you have already had a lot of experience with requirements, you might have found specific parts of the book helpful to perhaps improve certain aspects of your current approach to developing and managing your requirements.

In conclusion, you may wish to keep in mind three points of advice: (1) be confident, (2) never forget the human aspects and (3) decide on the right level of formality of the RM process and select the appropriate tools for your own context.

1. Be confident – this book contains all you need to know to do a good job of developing and managing your requirements effectively and efficiently, or have somebody professional do it for you if needed; no matter what your own context is.

2. Never forget the human aspects – you are surrounded by highly complex and unique individuals, with a tremendous range of gifts, skills and experience, different cultural backgrounds, as well as values and behaviors – yet we all have our faults and weaknesses. Unmotivated employees can have disastrous effects on any undertaking, whereas highly motivated employees are able

to achieve the most remarkable things. Employees are the most important assets of any company or project – treat them accordingly.

3.   Decide on the right level of formality of the RM process and select the appropriate tools for your own context – this will tremendously increase your efficiency, and it will also keep the people you work with motivated as they do not perceive to waste their efforts with an overly formal process and difficult tools.

This book was not intended to be an academic publication, but rather it was written to be a practical and realistic guide for anyone who would wish to make his requirements explicit, in order to ensure that his needs would be fully met – irrespective of the industry, the sector (public or private), the purpose of the organization (profit or not-for-profit) and the general context (work or leisure).

The contents of this book are based on a large variety of applied research, good practice, and hands-on experience across many industries. I trust you will have found reading this book useful, and perhaps even enjoyable. May this book contribute to your success – and become a helpful companion in your own personal quest for getting your requirements right.

Appendix A

Human Aspects – Dos and Don'ts

Dos	
Be upright and authentic	People will notice if you are not, and they won't believe you in the future. Also, if you are authentic, you will feel better during your work, and hence work better.
Show honest respect	Talk to and about everybody respectfully, whether they are around or not. People will notice, and there is nothing worse than to hear that someone you trust has talked badly about you behind your back. Make sure that you honestly respect people and do not just pretend.
Take people seriously	The people you work with are all professionals and each of them knows things you don't, and can do things you can't. Don't just respect them as human beings, but also as professionals.
Be open-minded	Sometimes the unexpected occurs and the person everybody thinks incapable of helping you, might just be the one who holds the information you need. You need to talk to people to find out, don't categorize them too quickly as unimportant or irrelevant for your work.
Create a climate of participation and ownership	Make the participants in the RM process feel that they actually participate and help to make progress. Honor and praise their contributions, giving them a feeling of ownership of what was achieved, and how it was achieved.
Share praise collectively (if things go well)	This will increase pride and ownership that the participants feel about the RM process and their contributions. And importantly, it will strongly motivate them to continue cooperating with you in the future.
Accept responsibility and shame personally (if things don't go well)	You are driving the RM process; the other participants contribute to your efforts. It is a strong sign of good leadership if you are great enough to take the blame and don't pass it on to the people who were trying to help you achieve.
Invest in your employees/ team members	If you are leading a team, the team members are your most precious assets. Without them you can't do the job. Against them you definitely won't be able to do the job. With them you can achieve things that you might not even imagine. Make sure they have the training they need, and importantly, they see that you also take their long-term career aspirations seriously, even if they are not directly related to your short-term RM work.

Empower your employees/ team members	If you send out your team members, give them the mandate and the support they need to do the work you expect them to do for you. Trust in them, and show them that you do. This will boost their motivation, as they will rightly feel valued and given responsibility.
Communicate well	Use stakeholders' languages if possible. Find out how they prefer to communicate and when it is most convenient for them. Make sure you never waste their time. Communicate in a concise way. Make sure they have correctly understood you and vice versa.
Consider yourself a service provider	Whether you are an internal employee or an external service provider for a program or project team, always try your best to deliver an excellent service in terms of RM. In larger scale programs or if you are indeed an external service provider, you absolutely should invest in the systematic management of your service quality.

Don'ts	
Don't be arrogant	You are dependent on the people you work with. Arrogance never creates trustful, respectful and amicable relationships. If you are an arrogant type of person, start working on yourself immediately. Try to improve – or look for a job where you don't have to work with people.
Don't be pushy	You should be careful never to push people around. It may work in the short run, but they will try to avoid you in the future.
Don't lie	One of the most devastating things you can do to prevent trust relationships is to lie. Once people find out you lie, they will turn away from you, which will make your work impossible or at least very difficult.
Don't talk badly behind peoples' backs	That is another 'reputation killer'. People are actually quite intelligent. When they see you 'slag off' other people behind their backs, they might wonder what you say about them behind theirs.
Don't claim successes personally	Only bad leaders and poor managers claim that the team achievements occurred solely due to their own doing. This sends a strong message to all who participated that their contributions really were worthless, and that the only person properly contributing was you yourself.
Don't blame others in case of failures	In some instances, this might even be worse than the above, especially if unjustified. Great leaders stand in front of their team and take the blame, if things did not work out as planned.
Don't speak RM jargon to people who are not familiar with it	Have you ever spoken to a 'fanatical' stamp collector (no offense if you are one of them)? Now imagine you have barely heard of RM, and your team's Requirements Manager sits on your desk and speaks in RM abbreviations ... Since you need information from the participants in the RM process, you should try to speak their own language (both technical and native), if you can.
Don't assume because you have said something, everybody has understood you	Have you ever had a misunderstanding in your own family, perhaps with your own spouse? Well, presumably you have known each other for some time and you talk about things you both know. Now think about how easily misunderstandings do occur with people you don't know that well in the workplace. This is a difficult trap to avoid, but it pays to make an effort.

Appendix B

Process Checklist – Requirements Development (RD)

Step 1 – Explore the context			
Workflow	**Activity**	**Input**	**Output**
Workflow 1.1 **Identify and review relevant documentation**	Identify and review relevant procedural documents	Relevant procedural documents	Relevant procedural documents identified and reviewed
	Identify and review relevant regulation and legislation	Relevant regulation and legislation	Relevant regulation and legislation identified and reviewed
	Identify and review relevant studies and publications	Relevant studies and publications	Relevant studies and publications identified and reviewed
	Identify and review relevant lessons learned and good practice	Relevant lessons learned and good practice	Relevant lessons learned and good practice identified and reviewed
	Identify and review requirements from relevant previous projects or programs	Relevant previous requirements	Reusable requirements identified and reviewed
	Identify and review existing input requirements from potential stakeholders	Existing input requirements	Input requirements identified and reviewed
	Record relevant key information and sources	Relevant documentation identified and reviewed	Relevant key information and sources recorded
Workflow 1.2 **Identify and map stakeholders**	Identify relevant stakeholders	Relevant key information Recommendations	Relevant stakeholders identified
	Identify relevant domain experts	Relevant key information Recommendations	Relevant domain experts identified
	Map the relevant stakeholders and domain experts	Relevant stakeholders and domain experts identified	Relevant stakeholders and domain experts mapped

Step 1 – Explore the context			
Workflow	**Activity**	**Input**	**Output**
Workflow 1.3 **Elicit and capture relevant context information**	Prepare sessions with relevant stakeholders and domain experts	Relevant stakeholders and domain experts mapped	Relevant stakeholders and domain experts invited to sessions
	Initiate the capture of context information based on the recorded relevant key information	Relevant key information and sources recorded	Initial context information captured
	Extend the captured context information with the relevant stakeholders and domain experts	Initial context information captured	Context information completed
	Document how the context information was extended by who until completion	Initial context information captured	Context information traceable to its sources

Step 2 – Identify the needs			
Workflow	**Activity**	**Input**	**Output**
Workflow 2.1 **Derive needs**	Establish a set of needs	Context information completed and traceable to its sources	Set of needs established
	Establish traceability from each need to the underlying context information	Set of needs established	Set of needs traceable to the underlying context information
Workflow 2.2 **Analyze and update needs**	Analyze each need individually	Set of needs established Traceability of needs established	Quality gaps of individual needs identified
	Update each need as needed	Quality gaps of individual needs identified	Needs updated individually
	Analyze the complete set of needs	Needs updated individually	Conflicts and duplications identified
	Update the complete set of needs as needed	Conflicts and duplications identified	Conflicts of needs documented Duplications of needs removed

Step 2 – Identify the needs			
Workflow	**Activity**	**Input**	**Output**
Workflow 2.3 **Validate needs**	Prepare the validation of the needs	Complete set of analyzed and updated needs	Relevant stakeholders and domain experts invited to sessions
	Drive the validation by the relevant stakeholders and domain experts	Relevant stakeholders and domain experts invited to sessions	Validation of needs completed
	Record the outcome of the validation	Validation of needs completed	Outcome of needs validation recorded
	Implement any necessary changes	Changes necessary as agreed during the validation of needs	Necessary changes implemented
	Record the implementation of any necessary changes	Necessary changes implemented	Implemented changes recorded

Step 3 – Establish the requirements			
Workflow	**Activity**	**Input**	**Output**
Workflow 3.1 **Create goal hierarchies**	Create a goal hierarchy for each validated need	A set of validated needs	One goal hierarchy per validated need
	Identify all root goals in all goal hierarchies	One goal hierarchy per validated need	All root goals identified
Workflow 3.2 **Analyze and update goal hierarchies**	Analyze each goal individually	Complete list of individual goals	Each goal analyzed individually
	Update each goal as needed	Each goal analyzed individually	Each individual goal updated as needed
	Analyze each goal hierarchy individually	All established goal hierarchies	Each goal hierarchy analyzed individually
	Update each goal hierarchy as needed	Each goal hierarchy analyzed individually	Each goal hierarchy updated as needed
	Analyze the complete set of goal hierarchies	Complete set of goal hierarchies	Complete set of goal hierarchies analyzed
	Update the complete set of goal hierarchies as needed	Complete set of goal hierarchies analyzed	Complete set of analyzed and updated goal hierarchies

Step 3 – Establish the requirements			
Workflow	**Activity**	**Input**	**Output**
Workflow 3.3 <u></u> **Validate goal hierarchies**	Prepare the validation of the goal hierarchies	Complete set of analyzed and updated goal hierarchies	Relevant stakeholders and domain experts invited to sessions
	Drive the validation by the relevant stakeholders and domain experts	Relevant stakeholders and domain experts invited to sessions	Validation of goal hierarchies completed
	Record the outcome of the validation	Validation of goal hierarchies completed	Outcome of the validation of goal hierarchies recorded
	Implement any necessary changes	Changes necessary as agreed during the validation of goal hierarchies	Necessary changes implemented
	Record the implementation of any necessary changes	Necessary changes implemented	Implemented changes recorded
Workflow 3.4 **Write requirements**	For each validated root goal write one new requirement or reuse a suitable existing requirement	Validated root goals Identified reusable requirements	Own requirements captured based on validated root goals
	For each identified input requirement write one new requirement or reuse a suitable existing requirement	Identified input requirements Identified reusable requirements	Own requirements captured based on input requirements
	Establish traceability from each new requirement and reused requirement to the respective source	Own requirements captured	Own requirements linked to sources
	Complete all mandatory attribute information for each new and reused requirement	Own requirements linked to sources	Own requirements completed

Step 3 – Establish the requirements			
Workflow	**Activity**	**Input**	**Output**
<u>Workflow 3.5</u> **Analyze and update requirements**	Analyze each own requirement individually	Own requirements completed	Quality gaps of individual requirements identified
	Update each own requirement as needed	Quality gaps of individual requirements identified	Own requirements updated individually
	Analyze the complete set of own requirements	Own requirements updated individually	Conflicts and duplications identified
	Resolve conflicts and duplications as needed with the concerned relevant stakeholders	Conflicts and duplications identified	All identified conflicts and duplications resolved
	Update own requirements as needed	All identified conflicts and duplications resolved	Own requirements updated
	Document the outcome of the analysis and the resolution of the identified conflicts and duplications	Own requirements updated	All updates documented
<u>Workflow 3.6</u> **Validate requirements**	Prepare the validation of the requirements	Complete set of analyzed and updated own requirements	Relevant stakeholders invited to sessions
	Drive the validation by the relevant stakeholders	Relevant stakeholders invited to sessions	Validation of requirements completed
	Record the outcome of the validation	Validation of requirements completed	Outcome of requirements validation recorded
	Implement any necessary changes	Changes necessary as agreed during the validation of requirements	Necessary changes implemented
	Record the implementation of any necessary changes	Necessary changes implemented	Implemented changes recorded

Appendix C

Process Checklist – Requirements Change Management (RCM)

Step 4 – Manage requirements change			
Workflow	**Activity**	**Input**	**Output**
Workflow 4.1 **Identify the need for change**	Identify the need for change from the perspective of the relevant stakeholders	Requirement change notification received from relevant stakeholder	Need for change due to changes of input requirements identified
	Identify the need for change from within the own domain	Update of relevant own domain knowledge	Need for change from within own domain identified
	Identify the need for change due to changes of the relevant regulation or legislation	Relevant change of regulation or legislation	Need for change due to changes in regulation or legislation identified
	Document the identified need for change	Need for change identified	Need for change documented
Workflow 4.2 **Analyze the impacts of the identified need for change**	Identify which own requirements are impacted by the identified need for change	Need for change documented	Own requirements identified that are potentially impacted
	Identify which own requirements will have to be changed	Own requirements identified that are potentially impacted	Own requirements identified that will have to be changed
	Categorize the needed change of own requirements	Own requirements identified that will have to be changed	Needed changes to own requirements categorized
	Document the outcome of the analysis	Needed changes to own requirements categorized	Outcome of impact analysis documented
Workflow 4.3 **Prepare the proposed change**	Formulate the proposed changes to own requirements	Outcome of impact analysis documented	Proposed changes to own requirements formulated
	Complete the documentation and traceability of the proposed changes	Proposed changes to own requirements formulated	Proposed changes documented and traced

Step 4 – Manage requirements change			
Workflow	**Activity**	**Input**	**Output**
Workflow 4.4 **Analyze the impacts of the proposed change**	Analyze the impacts of the proposed changes internally	Proposed changes documented and traced	Impacts analyzed internally
	Analyze the impact of the proposed changes externally	Proposed changes documented and traced	Impacts analyzed externally
	Identify any relevant change process (if applicable)	Impacts analyzed internally and externally	Applicable change process identified
	Document the outcome of the analysis	Applicable change process identified Change impacts analyzed	Outcome of impact analysis documented
Workflow 4.5 **Agree the proposed change**	Prepare the validation of the proposed changes	Outcome of impact analysis documented	Relevant stakeholders invited to sessions
	Drive the validation by the relevant stakeholders	Relevant stakeholders invited to sessions	Proposed changes to own requirements validated
	Record the outcome of the validation	Proposed changes to own requirements validated	Outcome of validation documented
	Implement any necessary changes	Outcome of validation documented	Necessary changes to the proposed changes implemented
	Record the implementation of any necessary changes	Necessary changes to the proposed changes implemented	Implementation of necessary changes recorded
Workflow 4.6 **Implement the agreed change**	Apply the agreed changes to own requirements	Changes to own requirements agreed	Agreed changes to own requirements applied
	Check that the agreed changes to own requirements have been applied as agreed	Agreed changes to own requirements applied	Application of the agreed changes checked
	Publish the new version of the requirements and trigger the relevant change process (if applicable)	Application of the agreed changes checked	Updated own requirements published Applicable change process triggered
	Check that the underlying need for change has been met	Application of the agreed changes checked	Need satisfaction checked

Appendix D

Tools Supporting Requirements Management (RD + RCM)

The following tools were referred to in Chapter 6. However, this selection of tools does not represent in any way the outcome of a comparative selection of all available tools that can support the RM process.

Many additional tools can be found on the market, both COTS tools and freeware or open source tools. The former are available for purchase, often with an extensive portfolio of support services and options to choose from. The latter can usually be used for free, but will often not come with any support services, nor do they tend to be of similar industrial maturity, and they may be updated rather frequently, outside your control.

Thus, for a given project or program, the selection of the tools to support RM has to be made depending on a number of factors, such as the existing IT infrastructure, specific needs or constraints of the project or program at hand, the level of relevant skills and experience among the people likely to work with these tools, the costs of making these tools available to the end users, the technical support offered, and so on. Chapter 6 provides a more detailed description of the intended contexts and purposes of these types of tools.

GATHERING AND STRUCTURING INFORMATION

- MindManager   by Mindjet [28]

- Excel   by Microsoft [27]

- MagicDraw   by No Magic [31]

- iMindMap   by ThinkBuzan [29]

- NovaMind   by NovaMind [30]

TRACING INFORMATION

- DOORS   by IBM [32]

- Cradle   by 3SL [33]

- RequisitePro   by IBM [34]

ANALYZING INFORMATION

- Requirements Quality Analyzer   by Re-use [35]

REPORTING AND DOCUMENTING INFORMATION

- PowerPoint   by Microsoft [27]

- Word   by Microsoft [27]

Appendix E

Requirements Quality Checklist (Individual Requirements)

Check that each individual requirement is:

Criteria	Comments
Necessary	Each requirement has to be necessary, that is, there has to be an identified stakeholder with an underlying, justified need. A requirement will have a certain priority, which can change over time. But even low priority requirements have to be necessary in the sense that they have to be stated. Think about what would be the worst that could happen if you left the requirement out.
Attainable	Each requirement has to be realistic and achievable in terms of the laws of physics and domain experience. Technical feasibility, as well as budget and schedule constraints should be considered, but they should not prevent you from stating challenging requirements. Often, in the beginning of a new program, the needed technologies to satisfy some of the requirements will not be available yet. If something is required it has to be stated as a requirement, even if we cannot satisfy it yet. At least this helps to make that very fact explicit.
Clear/Unambiguous	Requirements, in particular the requirement statements have to be clear and unambiguous, in order to avoid misunderstandings. They shall be kept as simple as possible, using relevant punctuation, consisting of only one sentence per requirement statement (and only one requirement per sentence), avoiding noun clusters and using tabular layout where appropriate.
Verifiable	For each requirement you should think about how the design, and later on the product should be verified, so that you can decide, whether you consider that the requirement has been satisfied. Therefore each requirement has to be formulated in a way that it is verifiable, and you should have proposed means of design and/or product verification in the corresponding attributes of the requirement.
Not Premature Design	The requirement should never constrain the solution space more than necessary at its level. Solutions should only be imposed by means of requirements, if this is really a constraint. For example, if a stakeholder explicitly needs a detailed specific solution for a justified reason.
Complete	Each requirement has to contain all needed statement components, mandatory attribute information, and links or references, in line with the established requirements data model.

Appendix F

Requirements Document Quality Checklist (Set Of Requirements)

A requirements document (= a set of requirements) shall be:

Criteria	Comments
Complete	All necessary requirements from all identified relevant stakeholders are present, and have been analyzed. All defined categories of requirements have been considered, and all identified scenarios, functions and use cases have been taken into account.
Consistent	No two requirements are in direct conflict. Any such conflicts have been identified, addressed and resolved by means of negotiation with the concerned relevant stakeholders (or escalated for a decision at a higher level).
Non-redundant	Each requirement is expressed only once in the document or set of requirements. There are no duplications, neither full nor partial duplications. Full duplications should lead to one of the duplicated requirements being deleted. Partial duplications are harder to spot and can often be resolved by combining concerned requirements.
Structured	There should be a clear structure within the requirements document. This structure can be based on one or several of the following criteria: system architecture, requirements type, work breakdown structure, project or program schedule, operational functions, system features, as well as identified scenarios and/or use cases. A good document structure is helpful because it facilitates the document's readability and analysis for completeness and consistency.
Validated	All requirements contained in the document have to be validated by the identified, relevant stakeholders. The owner or author of the document would have driven this validation process, and demonstrated to all relevant stakeholders that all quality criteria have been met, both at the individual requirements level and at the set of requirements level. The formal validation confirms that the relevant stakeholders agree that the requirements are correct, consistent and complete.
Approved	In many cases, a designated manager or commercial representative will have to formally approve a requirements document. In such cases, the approver will have made sure that all quality criteria are met for the entire document, before signing it off. Documents can also be approved in cases where not all requirements have been validated yet, for example to release a draft requirements document to a supplier or risk sharing partner.

Appendix G

Mapping of RM Workflows to Supporting Techniques and Tools

The following Matrix shows the recommended mapping of RM process workflows to supporting techniques and types of tools that was described in detail in Chapter 5 (from the workflow perspective) and in Chapter 6 (from the technique and tool perspective).

Techniques and Tools	Step 1 workflows			Step 2 workflows			Step 3 workflows						Step 4 workflows					
	1.1	1.2	1.3	2.1	2.2	2.3	3.1	3.2	3.3	3.4	3.5	3.6	4.1	4.2	4.3	4.4	4.5	4.6
Brain storming	X	X	X															
Mind mapping	X	X	X	X	X	X	X	X	X	X	X	X		X	X	X	X	X
Diagramming user interactions			X				X											
Functional analysis			X				X											
Safety analysis			X				X											
Why-why analysis			X				X											
Scenario analysis			X				X											
Use case analysis			X				X											
Walkthrough			X				X											
Establishing traceability				X			X			X								
Traceability analysis										X	X	X	X	X	X	X	X	X
Requirements quality analysis										X	X	X						
Presentation																	X	X
Reporting																		X
Mind mapping tool	X	X	X	X	X	X	X	X	X	X	X	X		X	X	X	X	X
Spreadsheet tool	X	X	X				X	X	X	X	X	X						
Modeling tool			X				X											
Object management tool										X	X	X	X	X	X	X	X	X
Requirements analysis tool										X	X	X						
Presentation tool																	X	X
Text editor tool																		X

Bibliography

[1]   Sommerville, I. 2007. *Software Engineering*. Pearson.

[2]   Alexander, I. and Stevens, R. 2002. *Writing Better Requirements*. Pearson.

[3]   Hooks, I.F. 1990. Why Johnny can't write requirements. AIAA conference.

[4]   Bahill, T. and Henderson, S. 2005. Requirements development, verification and validation exhibited in famous failures. *Systems Engineering*, 8(1), 1–14.

[5]   INCOSE. 2011. *Systems Engineering Handbook – A Guide for System Life CycleProcesses and Activities*. INCOSE SE Handbook Version 3.2.1.

[6]   Jackson, S. 1997. *Systems Engineering for Commercial Aircraft*. Ashgate.

[7]   Hull, E., Jackson, K. and Dick, J. 2002. *Requirements Engineering*. Springer.

[8]   Robertson, S. and J. 1999. *Mastering the Requirements Process*. Pearson.

[9]   Kotonya, G. and Sommerville, I. 1998. *Requirements Engineering: Processes and Techniques*. Wiley.

[10] http://www.standishgroup.com [last accessed 10 March 2012]

[11] Chatzoglou, P.C. and Macaulay, L. 1995. Requirements capture and analysis: A survey of current practice. *Communications of the ACM*, 38(5).

[12] Lucchetta, G., Baroni, M., Delaire, L. and Bariani, P.F. 2008. Aircraft requirements elicitation and development during conceptual design. University of Padova/Airbus, not published.

[13] Fricke, E. and Schulz, A. 2005. Design for changeability (DfC): Principles to enable changes in systems throughout their entire lifecycle. *Systems Engineering Journal*, 8(4), 342–359.

[14] Kossmann, M., Odeh, M. and Gillies, A. 2007. 'Tour d'horizon' in Requirements Engineering – Areas left for exploration. IS'07, INCOSE.

[15] Kossmann, M., Odeh, M., Gillies, A. and Wong, R. 2008. From process-driven to knowledge-driven Requirements Engineering using domain ontology. IS'08, INCOSE.

[16] Kossmann, M., Odeh, M., Gillies, A. and Watts, S. 2009. Ontology-Driven Requirements Engineering with reference to the aerospace industry. ICADIWT'09, IEEE.

[17]	http://www.bikeradar.com [last accessed 10 March 2012]

[18]	http://www.airbus.com [last accessed 10 March 2012]

[19]	Warwick, G. and Norris, G. 2010. Designs for Success: Systems Engineering Must be Rethought if Program Performance is to Improve. *Aviation Week & Space Technology*, 172(40), 72–75.

[20]	Hammer, M. and Stanton, S. 2000. Prozessunternehmen – wie sie wirklich funktionieren. *Harvard Business Manager*, 22(3), 68–81.

[21]	Kotter, J., Schlesinger, L.A. and Sathe, V. 1986. *Organization: On the Management of Organizational Design and Change*. Irwin.

[22]	Kotter, J. 1996. *Leading Change: Harvard Business School Press*. Penguin.

[23]	Palmer, A. 1994. *Principles of Services Marketing*. McGraw-Hill.

[24]	Zeithaml, V., Bitner, M. and Gremler, D. 2008. *Services Marketing*. McGraw-Hill.

[25]	Kossmann, M. 2006. *Delivering Excellent Service Quality in Aviation*. Ashgate.

[26]	Halligan, R. 2010. Requirements quality metrics: The basis of informed Requirements Engineering management. http://www.ppi-int.com/newsletter/SyEN-013.php [last accessed 10 March 2012]

[27]	http://office.microsoft.com [last accessed 10 March 2012]

[28]	http://www.mindjet.com [last accessed 10 March 2012]

[29]	http://www.thinkbuzan.com [last accessed 10 March 2012]

[30]	http://www.novamind.com [last accessed 10 March 2012]

[31]	https://www.magicdraw.com [last accessed 10 March 2012]

[32]	http://www-01.ibm.com/software/awdtools/doors [last accessed 10 March 2012]

[33]	http://www.threesl.com [last accessed 10 March 2012]

[34]	http://www-01.ibm.com/software/awdtools/reqpro [last accessed 10 March 2012]

[35]	http://www.reusecompany.com [last accessed 10 March 2012]

[36]	http://www.fondazionesofia.com [last accessed 10 March 2012]

[37]	http://www.airbus.com [last accessed 10 March 2012]

Index

3–D printing 35–6
3SL 125, 168

A350 XWB 34, 136, 148–51
A380 19–20
actual cost 46
additive layer manufacturing 36
Africa 138–9
Airbus 16, 19–21, 33–4, 38, 136,
    148–50
aircraft delivery center 151
aircraft development program 68, 74,
    148
Alexander 13, 175
analysis
    change impact 11, 114
    coverage 123
    derivation 123
    fault tree 121
    functional 84, 92, 121, 128, 173
    hazard 121
    impact 11, 111, 113–5, 123, 127,
        165
    particular risk 121
    requirements 173
    requirements quality 105–6, 108,
        123, 125, 131, 173
    safety 84, 121, 128, 173
    scenario 84, 92, 122, 128, 173
    traceability 106, 108, 111–6, 123,
        131, 173

use case 84, 92, 122, 128, 173
    why-why 84, 121, 128, 173
analyzing information 117, 126, 130–1
architecture
    solution 23
    system 100, 103–4, 121, 128, 171
Asia 138
assumptions 4, 52, 100, 102

Bahill 15, 175
Bariani 16, 175
Baroni 16, 175
brain storming 81–2, 84, 120, 127, 138,
    173
breakdown structure
    product 44
    system 51–2
    work 43–4, 46, 104, 171
business improvement project 41,
    43–4
business object model 123, 130

cash flow 45, 52
change control 14, 74, 111
change impact analysis 11, 114
Chatzoglou 15, 175
commercial off the shelf
    see COTS
communications
    word-of-mouth 65, 67–8, 118
competitive advantage 15, 108

completeness 13, 26, 38–9, 86, 91–2,
    101, 104, 107, 122–5, 128, 131, 171
complex system 15, 17, 19, 27, 37, 91,
    141–2, 144, 147–8
complexity
    system 8, 31, 135–6, 154
configuration management 21, 24,
    76, 148
consistency 13, 24, 26, 38–9, 86, 90–2,
    99, 104, 107, 122, 125, 128, 131,
    171
constraint 9, 12, 41, 66, 80, 86, 96–7,
    102, 122, 144–5, 167, 169
control
    change 14, 74, 111
corrective rework 10, 13, 17, 23, 25–6,
    30, 35, 52, 75, 77
correctness 13, 26, 38–9, 86, 92, 107,
    122, 125, 128, 131
cost
    actual 46
    non-recurring 14, 44, 52, 103
    recurring 14, 52, 103
cost management 42–5, 49, 52
COTS 35, 37, 102, 167
coverage analysis 123
Cradle 125, 168
criteria
    quality 105–6, 113, 171
customer expectations 13, 31, 33, 35,
    80
customer involvement 34
customer retention 65
customer turnover 65
cycle
    life
        development 29, 30, 37, 49, 150
        entire 14, 17, 21, 24, 29, 42,
            48–9, 52, 74, 103, 108
        operational 29, 37, 48

service quality 67

dashboard 124
data integrity 103, 149
data protection 149
data security 149
Delaire 16, 175
Democratic Republic of the Congo
    136, 143
derivation analysis 123
design process 23
design verification 22–3, 100, 107,
    150, 163
development
    product 16, 26, 35, 38
    requirements 8, 14, 23, 74–6, 78,
        84, 87, 89, 93, 101, 107, 109, 114,
        154, 159, 175
    system 9–10, 13, 17, 27, 37, 41, 45,
        56, 74, 81, 102
development life cycle 29–30, 37, 49,
    150
diagramming user interaction 84, 92,
    121, 127, 173
Dick 175
disposal 14, 20–1, 29, 48, 81
documenting information 117, 126,
    132–3, 168
DOORS 125, 148–9, 168, 176
DOORS Data Exchange 149
DOORS RMF 148
driven
    knowledge 16–7, 73, 153, 175
    process 16–7, 73
drum beating 56
duplication 61–2, 87, 90, 92–3, 104,
    106, 160, 163, 171

earned value 46
earned value management 43, 45, 48

emerging properties 22
enabling product 15, 99, 151
engineering
    requirements 14, 16, 175–6
    software 9, 14, 20, 22, 64, 175
    systems, *see* SE
engineering change proposal 110
entire life cycle 14, 17, 21, 24, 29, 42,
        48–9, 52, 74, 103, 108
establishing traceability 85, 123, 173
Europe 138
Excel 124, 167
extended enterprise 22, 24, 27, 29,
        32, 46, 52, 73–4, 98, 129, 131,
        147–50

fault tree analysis 121
final assembly line 33, 151
formality 11, 24, 135, 154–5
France 148
freeware 167
Fricke 16, 175
functional analysis 84, 92, 121, 128, 173

generic RM process 74–6, 153
Germany 148
goal hierarchy 90–2, 161

hazard analysis 121
Henderson 15, 175
highly complex system 21, 73, 95,
        147, 153
Hooks 13, 175
Hull 175
human factors 8, 55, 57, 69, 153
human resource management 42–4,
        51

IBM 125, 148, 168, 176
iMindmap 124, 167

impact analysis 11, 111, 113–5, 123,
        127, 165
implementation strategies 61
India 148
industrial system 19, 31, 51, 151
information
    analyzing 117, 126, 130–1, 168
    documenting 117, 126, 132–3, 168
    gathering 117, 126–7, 167
    reporting 117, 126, 132–3, 168
    structuring 117, 120, 126–7, 167
    traceability 14, 29, 74, 76–7, 108
    tracing 117, 126, 129–30, 168
interview
    structured 118
    unstructured 118
IT infrastructure 167
IS/IT project 41, 46–7

Jackson 175

Katanga 143
key performance indicators 46, 57, 124
Kinshasa 143
knowledge driven 16–7, 73, 153, 175
Kotonya 175

Lubumbashi 143
Lucchetta 16, 175

Macaulay 15, 175
MagicDraw 125, 167, 176
management
    configuration 21, 24, 76, 148
    cost 42–5, 49, 52
    earned value 43, 45, 48
    human resource 42–4, 51
    material resource 42–4, 51
    non-compliance 23, 26, 129, 140,
        146

non-conformance 23
process 59
project 41–2, 46, 49, 52, 139, 153
project & program 6, 11, 41–2, 49,
    153
program 6, 11, 41–2, 49, 153
requirements change 8, 74–6, 78,
    84, 89, 108–9, 154, 165
risk and opportunity 42–3, 45, 52,
    147
schedule 42–3, 45, 49, 51
service quality 68
supplier 42–3, 46, 49, 52
marketing mix 65–6
material resource management 42–4,
    51
Microsoft 124–6, 167–8, 176
mind mapping 81–2, 84–5, 92–4,
    105–6, 108, 112–4, 120, 127, 173
mind mapping tool 85, 112–4, 124,
    127–8, 130–1, 137, 142, 173
MindJet 124, 167, 176
MindManager 124, 167
model
    business object 123, 130
    requirements data 97, 123, 130–1,
        169
modeling 22
modeling language
    system, see SysML
    unified, see UML
modeling tool 125, 127–8, 173
modification 14, 26, 29, 41, 48–9, 52,
    62
modification project 41, 49
monitoring and control 42–3, 46, 52,
    57, 130

New York 136, 138–40
No Magic 125, 167

non-compliance management 23, 26,
    129, 140, 146
non-conformance management 23
non-product 151
non-recurring cost 14, 44, 52, 103
NovaMind 124, 167, 176

object management tool 125, 131, 173
ontology 16, 175
open source tool 167
operational life cycle 29, 37, 48
operational scenario 101, 103, 122
opportunities 22, 31, 45, 50, 52, 63,
    82, 122, 140

particular risk analysis 121
planned value 46
PowerPoint 125, 168
presentation 115–6, 123–6, 132, 173
presentation tool 115–6, 124–6, 132,
    173
primary system 151
problem space 85–6
process
    design 23
    generic RM 74–6, 153
process driven 16–7, 73
process management 59
process organization 59–60
process owner 59
product breakdown structure 44
product development 16, 26, 35, 38
product validation 22–3
product verification 23, 97, 100, 169
profit margin 30, 35
project
    business improvement 41, 43–4
    IS/IT 41, 46–7
    modification 41, 49
    research 16

system development 27, 37, 45, 102
project management 41–2, 46, 49, 52, 139, 153
project & program management *see* P&PM
program management 6, 11, 41–2, 49, 153
P&PM 6, 11, 41–2, 49, 153

Qualification 11
quality criteria 105–6, 113, 171

RCM 8, 14, 74–6, 78, 84, 89, 108–9, 154, 165
RD 8, 14, 23, 74–6, 78, 84, 87, 89, 93, 101, 107, 109, 114, 154, 159, 175
recurring cost 14, 52, 103
reporting 116–7, 124, 126, 131–3, 144–5, 168, 171
requirement
functional 9, 15, 100, 103, 121–2
legal 103, 142
non-functional 9–10, 15, 99
non-product 151
product 10, 151
requirement attribute 99, 112
requirement change note 110
requirement statement 96–9, 112, 123, 169
requirement type 99
requirements allocation 80, 100
requirements analysis 173
requirements cascade 123, 125, 150–1
requirements change management *see* RCM
requirements data model 97, 123, 130–1, 169
requirements development *see* RD

requirements document 6, 8, 79, 95, 98–9, 102, 104–5, 124–6, 150, 154, 171
requirements engineering 14, 16, 175–6
requirements manager 4, 11, 17–8, 57–8, 72, 74, 142, 148, 154, 158
requirements quality analysis 105–6, 108, 123, 125, 131, 173
Requirements Quality Analyzer 125, 168
requirements traceability 101
requirements validation 23, 100, 107, 150, 163
RequisitePro 125, 168
research project 16
resistance 55, 59–62
re-use 35, 73, 80, 85, 94–5, 101, 105, 130, 162
Re-use (company) 127, 168, 176
rework
corrective 10, 13, 17, 23, 25–6, 30, 35, 52, 75, 77
risk and opportunity management 42–3, 45, 52, 147
risk sharing partner 29, 32, 46, 52, 105, 149–50, 171
risks 23, 37, 45–6, 52, 80, 100, 122, 128–9, 136, 142, 146, 149
Robertson 175
role 6, 17, 19, 22, 31, 38, 41, 50, 52, 60, 62–3, 101, 153
roman catholic 140, 143

safety analysis 84, 121, 128, 173
Salvatorian 143
scenario analysis 84, 92, 122, 128, 173
schedule management 42–3, 45, 49, 51
Schulz 16, 175

SE 6, 19, 21, 30, 153, 175–6
series aircraft 151
served system 20–1, 102, 121, 127
service provider 68–9, 71, 158
serving system 20–1
service quality 33, 65–9, 71, 158, 176
service quality cycle 67
service quality management 68
set of requirements 41, 76, 82, 94–5,
    101, 104–8, 113, 171
simple system 8, 73, 136–7, 153
SOFIA 143–4, 146, 176
solution architecture 23
solution space 86, 97, 169
Sommerville 9–10, 175
space
    problem 85–6
    solution 86, 97, 169
Spain 148
spreadsheet tool 81–2, 92–4, 106, 108,
    124, 127–8, 130–1, 173
software engineering 9, 14, 20, 22, 64,
    175
Stevens 13, 175
structure
    breakdown
        product 44
        system 51–2
        work 43–4, 46, 104, 171
structured interview 118
structuring information 117, 120,
    126–7, 167
supplier management 42–3, 46, 49, 52
supply network 27, 150
SysML 121, 125
system
    complex 15, 17, 19, 27, 37, 91,
        141–2, 144, 147–8
    highly complex 21, 73, 95, 147,
        153

industrial 19, 31, 51, 151
    primary 151
    served 20–1, 102, 121, 127
    serving 20–1
    simple 8, 73, 136–7, 153
    transportation 20, 151
system architecture 101, 103–4, 121,
    128, 171
system breakdown structure 51–2
system complexity 8, 31, 135–6, 154
system development 9–10, 13, 17, 27,
    37, 41, 45, 56, 74, 81, 102
system development project 27, 37,
    45, 102
system modeling language
    see SysML
systems engineering
    see SE

Telelogic 148
testing 11, 37–8, 151
text editor tool 116, 124, 126, 133, 173
ThinkBuzan 124, 167, 176
tool
    freeware 165
    mind mapping 85, 112–4, 124,
        127–8, 130–1, 137, 142, 173
    modeling 125, 127–8, 173
    object management 125, 131, 173
    open source 167
    presentation 115–6, 123–6, 133,
        173
    spreadsheet 81–2, 92–4, 106, 108,
        124, 127–8, 130–1, 173
    text editor 116, 124, 126, 133, 173
Toulouse 148
traceability analysis 106, 108, 111–6,
    123, 131, 173
traceability information 14, 29, 74,
    76–7, 108

tracing information 117, 126, 129–30, 168
transportation system 20, 171

UML 121, 125
Unified Modeling Language
    see UML
United Nations 12, 42, 139
University of the West of England 16
unstructured interview 118
USA 138, 148
US Homeland Security 140
use case 84, 92, 101, 103–4, 121–2, 125, 128, 171, 173
use case analysis 84, 92, 122, 128, 173

validation
    product 22–3
    requirements 23, 100, 107, 150, 163
validation and verification 14–5, 17, 21, 23, 74

validation and verification activities 14, 74
validation and verification data 17
value
    earned 46
    planned 46
verification
    design 22–3, 100, 149–50
    product 23, 97, 100, 169
viewpoint 11–2, 37, 66, 92, 117, 125, 127, 132

walkthrough 84, 92, 122, 128, 173
why-why analysis 84, 121, 128, 173
Word 126, 168
word-of-mouth communications 65, 67–8, 118
work breakdown structure 43–4, 46, 104, 171
work package 38, 46, 149–51
workshop 25, 117, 119–20, 124, 138